THE ARMCHAIR TRAVELLER SERIES

BRAZIL
on the
MOVE

John Dos Passos

BRAZIL

on the

MOVE

(*Paragon House*) 1991.

NEW YORK

First Paperback edition, 1991

Published in the United States by

Paragon House Publishers
90 Fifth Avenue
New York, NY 10011

Published by arrangement with Doubleday, a
division of Bantam Doubleday Dell Publishing
Group, Inc.

Library of Congress Cataloging-in-Publication Data

Dos Passos, John, 1896-1970.
   Brazil on the move / John Dos Passos. — 1st
paperback ed.
      p.   cm. — (The Armchair traveller series)
   Reprint. Originally published: Garden City, N.Y. :
Doubleday, 1963.
      ISBN 1-55778-359-4 : $10.95
      1. Brazil—Description and travel—1951-1980.
2. Brazil—History.   3. Dos Passos, John, 1896-
1970—Journeys—Brazil.   I. Title.   II. Series.
F2516.D66   1991   90-39886
981—dc20   CIP

Manufactured in the United States of America
10 9 8 7 6 5 4 3 2 1

CONTENTS

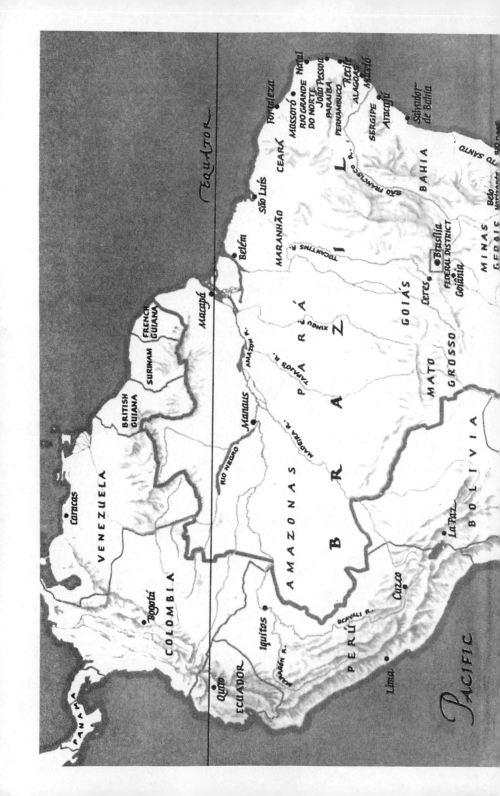

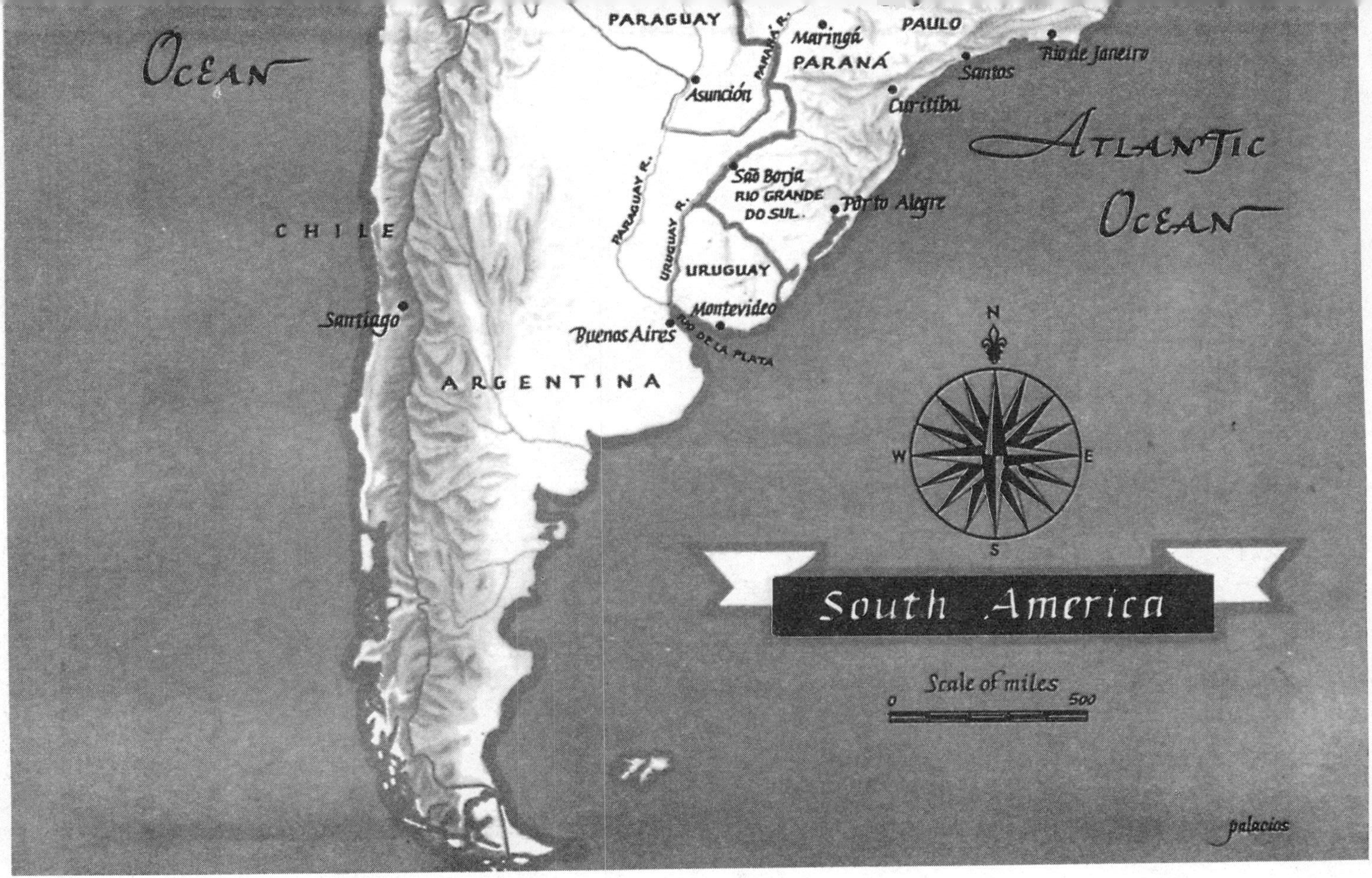
Ocean
PARAGUAY
PAULO
Maringá
PARANÁ
PARANÁ R.
Rio de Janeiro
Santos
Asunción
Curitiba
Atlantic
Ocean
São Borja
RIO GRANDE
DO SUL
Pôrto Alegre
PARAGUAY R.
URUGUAY R.
CHILE
URUGUAY
Santiago
Montevideo
Buenos Aires
RIO DE LA PLATA
ARGENTINA
N
W
E
S
South America
Scale of miles
0
500
palacios

BRAZIL
on the
MOVE

I

MELTING POT OF THE AMERICAS

The Brazilians are great people for telling stories on themselves. One story that was going the rounds a few years ago was about God and an archangel on the third day of creation. When the Lord Jehovah has finished making Brazil he can't help bragging a little to one of the archangels. He's planted the greatest forests and laid out the world's biggest river system and built a magnificent range of mountains with lovely bays and ocean beaches. He's filled the hills with topaz and aquamarine and sowed the rivers with gold dust and diamonds. He's arranged a climate free from hurricanes and earthquakes which will grow every conceivable kind of fruit.

"Is it fair, Lord," asks the archangel, "to give so many benefits to just one country?"

"You wait," says the Lord Jehovah, "till you see the people I'm going to put there."

The real point of this story is, of course, that it's topsy-turvy. Ever since the Portuguese founded their first colonies there in the early fifteen hundreds the development of Brazil has been held back by its inconvenient geography. The rivers run the wrong way. The mountains are in the wrong places. The steep coastal range for centuries formed a barrier to penetration of the interior. Though the central and southern uplands are suitable for colonization the rain forests of the Amazon basin in the north offer the sort of climate and terrain that no civilization has yet been able to cope with. The eastern bulge is cursed with perennial droughts. Until the coming of air transportation, which a Brazilian named Santos-Dumont, by the way, did almost as much as the Wright brothers to promote, it literally took months to get from one part of the country to the other. Tropical diseases are still a threat to development. The chief asset of Brazil is the Brazilians.

How did a handful of settlers from tiny Portugal, a country which during the great period of Portuguese colonization numbered at most a couple of million souls, manage to occupy and assimilate one half of the South American continent? How is it that the Brazilians, of all the South American peoples, seem furthest on the way towards producing a civilization of their own?

It is only recently that we have begun to recognize that there is something a little special about the colonial society the Portuguese established in America and Africa and the Orient. "Corrupt and inefficient" was what we were taught about it in school. The Portuguese have had, and continue to have, a bad press.

Perhaps the thread of racial and religious and political tolerance that keeps reappearing in their history has something to do with the success of the Portuguese as colonizers. To begin with Portugal was made up of more various cultural strains than the other colonizing nations of Europe.

The northern Portuguese had a lot of Celt in them. Many of the landowning families were the offspring of blueeyed Visigoths. There was a strong infusion of Burgundian French during the period of the establishment of the monarchy. In the south there was Arab and Berber blood. There, the peasantry, though Christian in religion, retained habits and customs acquired during three centuries of subjection to the Moors. The towns had a large Jewish population, possibly descended as much from Phoenician and Carthaginian colonists whose language and culture were Hebraic, as from the Israelites proper. During Portugal's formative years, each of these populations intermarried fairly freely with the rest.

The Spanish philosopher Miguel de Unamuno used to tell an amusing story to illustrate the prevalence of Semitic blood among the Portuguese. When the great King Manoel of Portugal wanted to marry a Spanish princess he was told that he must first purge his kingdom of Jews. He consented, but according to Don Miguel, the chief minister who brought the King the expulsion decree to sign, is supposed to have asked: "Which of us shall leave first, sire, you or me?"

Seafaring peoples tend to get their prejudices rubbed off. Farmland was scarce on the steep Portuguese coast. Its people were forced to find their livelihood in trading and fishing. Their wine trade with England ripened early into a political and commercial alliance which added one more element to their cosmopolitan outlook. Prince Henry the Navigator was a grandson of John of Gaunt. Then, after Vasco da Gama's rounding of the Cape of Good Hope, African slaves, and all the arts and complexities of India and China and Japan started pouring into Lisbon. Portuguese culture flared up into the sudden brilliance of the poetry of Camões and the surrealist style of the Manueline architects and stonecarvers.

It was at this explosive moment in the year 1500 that Pedro Alvares Cabral, in sailing a westerly course on his passage to India to avoid the calms off Africa that had so baffled Vasco da Gama, found himself, quite by accident, in Brazil.

A certain amount of mystery still hangs over the early exploration of the American coast. It is likely that even before Columbus's four expeditions opened up the New World to the Spaniards, Portuguese ships had been fetching the red dyewood called brazilwood from the beaches of the eastern bulge of South America. Brazil appeared on early maps as an Atlantic island.

When Cabral's little fleet sailed into Pôrto Seguro he seems to have taken it for granted that it was this island he was landing on. He celebrated Mass; announced to the Indians lurking about that he was taking possession in the name of Dom Manoel the First, King of Portugal and Lord of the Conquest, Navigation and Commerce of India, Ethiopia, and Persia; and sailed away to round the Cape of Good Hope in search of the profitable cargoes of spices he was hoping for in the Orient.

For a couple of centuries the authorities in Lisbon considered the settlements which grew up along the Brazilian coast, through the efforts of Jesuit missionaries and of private adventurers, as mere waystations to the East. Left to their own devices, marrying into Indian tribes for lack of Portuguese women, the colonists began to think of themselves as Brazilians.

In the north they raised sugar, and as the Indians were nomadic woodland hunters who couldn't adapt to agriculture, they imported slaves from Africa to plant and cut the cane.

In the backlands they raised cattle. As the population increased the need for fresh pastures and the perennial quest for gold drove the ranchers of the São Paulo plateau to scour the hinterland. Fighting or absorbing the Indians as they moved, they formed themselves into wandering bands that explored the country south to the La Plata estuary and west through the central uplands into the furthest confines of Mato Grosso. *Bandeirantes*, flagcarriers they called themselves.

When the Brazilians began to ship home gold and diamonds, the Portuguese kings woke up to the fact that Brazil was a valuable possession. Their oriental empire was falling to pieces. During the eighteenth century it was gold and precious stones from Brazil that supported the court at Lisbon.

The home government did little in return, except to try to keep the Brazilians in their place. After the expulsion of the Jesuits, schools and colleges were discouraged. Printing presses were forbidden, and so was any industry which might compete with the home country. Although British shipmasters already had a share in the Brazilian trade, it all had to be channeled through Lisbon.

When the Brazilians, particularly the prospectors and placerminers of Minas Gerais, heard that the English-speaking colonists in North America had thrown off the European yoke, they were moved to do likewise.

The earliest record I know of a political relationship between Brazil and English-speaking America is in Jefferson's report to John Jay when Jay was handling foreign affairs for the Continental Congress, of a conversation he had at Nîmes with a Brazilian medical student. It was in the spring of 1787. Jefferson was Minister to France. He had managed to break away from the gray drizzle of Paris for a breath of sunlight in the Midi. The Brazilian was named José Joaquim de Mayo. He seems to have been a member of a group in Rio affiliated with Tiradentes and his friends in the province of Minas Gerais. These later became known as the *Inconfidentes*, those disloyal to the King. De Mayo was asking whether the Brazilians could get help from North America if they set up an independent republic.

Jefferson had to tell him that the Confederated States had only been independent for five years, and that they were much too busy with domestic problems—it was only in the coming summer that the forty odd delegates were to shut themselves up in Philadelphia to write the constitution which cemented the Union—to engage in military adventures; and that, besides, their commercial relations with Portugal were profitable and cordial.

But liberty was still his passion. Jefferson couldn't help adding that "a successful revolution in Brasil could not be uninteresting to us. that prospects of lucre might possibly draw numbers of individuals to their aid, and purer motives our officers, among whom there are many excellent"; so he reported to Jay. Always the teacher, Jefferson went on to give the young Brazilian a little lesson in civil liberties. He explained that "our citizens being free to leave their own country individually without consent of their governments, are equally free to go to any other."

Reading over the scanty record of this meeting in the drapery-hung parlor of some stuffy French inn among the Roman ruins of Nîmes, you got the feeling that Jefferson and De Mayo had no need to waste time defining their terms. In spite of their bad French they understood each other. The libertarians of the eighteenth century spoke an international language.

The revolutionary movement of the *Inconfidentes* was crushed. A few years later Brazil attained independence in a quite different way from any other of the American nations.

Instead of being an exploited colony Brazil suddenly found itself the head and front of the Portuguese empire. This was in 1807. Although the British had destroyed French and Spanish seapower at Trafalgar, Napoleon's armies were sweeping Europe. In Portugal local republicans were greeting them with cheers. When the French advanced on Lisbon the ruling Bragança embarked his whole administration on a fleet said to have been of a thousand sail, and, under the protection of a British squadron, took off for Brazil.

For sixteen years he reigned in Rio as John VI of the Kingdoms of Portugal, Brazil, and the Algarve. Brazil developed mightily. The ports were opened to world commerce. European immigrants came in. A university was established. Printing presses were set up. Exiled French academicians started a school of fine arts. British soldiers and sailors trained the armed services. European investors set up industries. Rio took on a cosmopolitan cast it has never lost. Exports of sugar and forest products soared. Cattleraising flourished. The ranchers and the slaveowning sugar planters ran the country.

When the Braganças were restored to the Portuguese throne after Napoleon's abdication the Brazilians refused to go back to a colonial status. They set up John VI's son Dom Pedro I as constitutional emperor of an independent Brazil. When he failed to suit them, they sent him packing off to Portugal, and chose his son Dom Pedro II, still a small boy, to succeed him.

Dom Pedro II grew up to be an extraordinarily able ruler. He had the statesman's knack. Personally an unassuming man of scholarly tastes, he dedicated his life to developing responsible parliamentary government on the English model. The fifty years of his administration consolidated the Portuguese-speaking settlements spread over such an enormous terrain into a unified nation. It was largely due to Dom Pedro's foresight and moderation that while Spanish America split up after independence into turbulent and warring regimes, Portuguese America enjoyed comparative internal peace. When he was forced to abdicate in 1889 in favor of a federal republic, he went into exile leaving behind him among his beloved Brazilians habits of compromise and moderation in political affairs quite alien to the violence of the Spanish tradition. He was truly the father of his country.

The transition from monarchy to republic took place virtually without bloodshed. Though the Brazilian republic has suffered its share since then of the uprisings and pronunciamentos and military dictatorships that have until recent years been the rule in Latin America, the Brazilians have retained a respect for the legal way of doing things that seems more English than Mediterranean. Transitions from one regime to the other have tended to be by compromise instead of by violence. Brazil is a country of gusty oratory, but the bark of the politicians has usually proved worse than their bite.

There was an amusing instance of typically Brazilian moderation several years ago during Secretary of State Dulles' visit to Rio. The Communists controlled the national students' organization. Since hatred of the United States is their gospel, the leaders breathed fire and brimstone in an effort to stir up disagreeable incidents. Meanwhile the government and the more moderate factions among university students worked quietly to have everything smooth and rosy. The headquarters of the Communist students' organization turned out to be on the one road in from the airport. Never would they allow warmonger Dulles to pass their headquarters, they kept proclaiming. When the fateful day came Mr. Dulles was driven without incident past a building draped in black. The Communist students had moved their headquarters to a back street.

Along with this knack for political moderation, Brazil offers a picture of racial tolerance rather unusual in the world. This too is part of the Portuguese inheritance. Although slavery was not abolished there until the 1870s, the history of the relationship between master and slave has been different than among the English-speaking peoples.

The Portuguese were a mixed lot to begin with. Their long intercourse with the Moslems of North Africa resulted in a certain tolerance of polygamy at variance with their Christian faith. During their great expansion in the fifteenth and sixteenth centuries the Portuguese adventurers and navigators established footholds not only in Brazil but on both coasts of Africa, in Abyssinia and Persia and India and China and as far east as Japan, where it was Portuguese priests who introduced the Christian religion.

Though their appetite for expansion was enormous their numbers were few. Portugal was months and years of slow sailing away from the outposts of empire. They picked up their wives where they could. Indeed the Portuguese adventurers seem to have taken a naïve pride in the acquisition of the greatest possible number of wives and concubines from among the local populations. The Brazilian settlers particularly were family men with a vengeance. Even today it is not uncommon to find a Brazilian supporting several families. Bastards of various hues were considered members of the family.

The Portuguese family was patriarchal in the Biblical sense. In Brazil, as in the Old Testament, the patriarch had power of life and death over every member of the family group. At the same time he was responsible for their welfare. When the scarcity of hands, in the homeland as well as in the colonies, was remedied by the importation of Negro slaves, slaves were considered part of the family, as they are in Arabia today. The master's mulatto children enjoyed a certain status. Half-breeds, whether of Indian or Negro blood, tended to be drawn into the dominant culture, instead of being discarded into an outcast class as they were in English-speaking America. The social results of this difference in attitude have been tremendous.

There has resulted a society where racial tensions are few. As early as colonial times the Jews discovered so little prejudice against them that they had trouble preserving their cultural identity. After a couple of generations of intermarriage they melted away into the rest of the population. The same thing seems to be happening to the Germans and Italians who colonized the southern states and to recent European immigrants pouring into Rio and São Paulo. There is an amoebalike quality about the mild Portuguese culture which absorbs the most diverse elements.

The growing diversity in the national origins of the Brazilians shows up in public life. One of the leading politicians is ex-President Kubitschek. Oscar Niemeyer is their best-

known architect. The pioneer in modern architecture at São
Paulo was named Warschavchik. Rio's famous afterluncheon
speaker is named Herbert Moses. Particularly in São Paulo
you meet families with North American surnames that date
back to the southern slaveholders who emigrated to Brazil
after the Civil War. There are Smiths who don't speak a word
of English. Even the Japanese, established at first in tightly
exclusive colonies, are beginning to melt into the population.

The patriarchal mentality, combining with the humane
impulses of the European nineteenth century, produced during the last fifty years an attitude of tenderness towards the
Stone Age peoples of the Brazilian forests. In that period
Brazil was a leader in the effort to conciliate and preserve
primitive peoples.

It's worth noting that one of Brazil's great military heroes
was Candido Rondón, who died a field marshal at the ripe
old age of ninetytwo. Rondón was three fourths Indian. His
paternal grandfather was a bandeirante out of São Paulo who
settled in Mato Grosso and married a Terena Indian. His
mother was a Bororó. From the day he entered a military
school back in the days of the empire, throughout his long
and successful military career, he devoted his great energies
to the gradual civilizing of the forest Indians. Like his bandeirante grandfather Rondón was irresistibly attracted to the
rainforests and the jungles. He personally mapped and sur-
veyed more undiscovered territory than any Brazilian of his
time. It was Rondón who shepherded Theodore Roosevelt
during the exploring trip to the River of Doubt that was
nearly the end of T.R.

The Indian Protection Service Rondón set up is unique.
He worked out a battery of methods for civilizing the wild
tribes without destroying them. At the same time his Bound-
ary Commission to map the disputed frontiers with the
Guianas and Venezuela and Colombia accomplished miracles in eliminating international friction. Rondón managed

to replace nationalist fanaticism by a spirit of rational give and take. "Never be the first to shoot," was his motto.

Along with racial toleration, religious toleration has been the rule. Although Brazil is predominantly Catholic it is one of the few South American countries where Protestant missionaries are not interfered with. The Inquisition never reached Brazil. For a century there religious toleration has been so complete that the average Brazilian city offers today almost as many religious sects as Los Angeles. Alongside of the predominant Catholics you find Episcopalians, evangelistic Protestants of every stripe, Christian Scientists, followers of Auguste Comte, spiritualists, and votaries of various African cults brought over by the slaves. In the thoroughly uptodate city of Pôrto Alegre in Rio Grande do Sul we found a half voodoo, half spiritualist group called The White Line of Umbanda announcing its meetings in the newspapers.

As the threat of a Communist-colored dictatorship looms ever larger, the votaries of the most various religious sects tend to draw together. The last time I was in Rio I attended a meeting organized by a league for the defense of civil liberties. A large crowd, made up of the most diverse elements among rich and poor, gathered on the open lawn between the ranks of great trees that form the square behind what is known as Russell Beach on Guanabara Bay. The Catholic archbishop of Niterói, a number of church dignitaries, several Protestant ministers, a positivist, a representative of the spiritualists and a Jewish rabbi spoke from the same platform.

The rabbi's speech was one of the most touching I have ever heard. He told of the oppressions and miseries of his early life in Russia and Poland, the constant harassment on account of his race and his religion, the agony of the escape and the delight of landing in the new world of Brazil. He had been received with hospitality, and with a sort of inattentive friendliness that could hardly be called toleration, because the

Brazilians saw nothing particular about him that needed to be tolerated. He was a man like themselves. He spoke with pride and gratitude of his Brazilian citizenship. Only in Brazil had he come to understand the meaning of freedom.

II

THE PEOPLE THE LORD PUT THERE

Travels with a Studebaker

I first landed off an airplane in Rio back in 1948 when I was on a South American tour to do some articles for *Life*. Bill and Connie White, who were then running the *Life-Time* bureau in that part of the world, let out that they were starting next morning to drive their Studebaker up into the hinterland of Minas Gerais (the state of "assorted mines"), which lies to the north of the mountain barrier that hems in the city of Rio de Janeiro and the great bay of Guanabara. I snatched at the opportunity to take a peep into the back country before getting tangled up with the capital city. Their faces certainly fell when I asked them if they would mind if I came along. They'd been planning a private expedition on their own. They mumbled a reluctant yes. As it turned out the trip was a success all around. None of us ever laughed so much in our lives.

The roads were rough. The hotels were worse. At a place named Conselheiro Lafaiete the only lodging we could find seemed to be built over a railroad roundhouse. Smoke and steam from the engines occasionally came up through the floor. In one room there was an open manhole that threatened to drop you into some black pit below. We'd barely got settled

round a rickety table in the bare loft and were pouring ourselves out a drink when the electric lights went off. That
meant every light in town. The streets were deep in mud.
To find the local restaurant we had to grope our way along
the walls in the dark.

The eating place turned out to be a sort of saloon lit by
kerosene lamps. There was a rough noisy crowd, railroad section hands mostly. At that time, in spite of my Portuguese
name, I was still trying to communicate with people in Spanish. In Conselheiro Lafaiete nobody understood a word, but
they didn't show the slightest surprise or annoyance at having three foreigners come crawling in out of the dark. They
made us feel at home. The meal was mostly beans and rice
and those not of the best, but the proprietor served up the
dishes with a sort of flourish that made them seem better
than they were. We got the feeling we were eating quite a
blue ribbon dinner. We had a wonderful evening. By the time
we made our way back to our uncertain couches in the self-
styled hotel we felt we knew something about the people there
and that they knew something about us. Don't ask me how.
We'd made friends.

It's always been like this. I can't help a sort of family feeling for the Brazilians. Perhaps the fact that I had a Portuguese grandfather helps account for it. When people ask me
why I keep wanting to go to Brazil, part of the answer is that
it's because the country is so vast and so raw and sometimes
so monstrously beautiful; but it's mostly because I find it easy
to get along with the people.

We turned off the road to see the baroque pilgrimage
church at Congonhas do Campo. The shrines at Congonhas
are full of the work of a very local sculptor known as Aleijadinho (the little cripple), who lived in the late eighteenth
century. Working a soft soapstonelike rock, Aleijadinho developed an extreme form of baroque expressionism. In the

carving of the Stations of the Cross along the steep steps
that lead up 'to the main church, and in the saints and
martyrs of its gravely balanced façade, he pushed senti-
mentality beyond bathos, into a realm of ecstasy reminiscent
of El Greco's painting. Joy, sadness, pain, always pain, come
through with physical intensity. Some of the stone saints
seem, as certain miracleworking images are supposed to do, to
weep real tears.

The steps that led up to the church were thronged with
countrypeople who had vowed the pilgrimage. Some climbed
on their knees. Along the fringes sat beggars and old men
and cowled women selling fruit and trinkets and little meat
pies. The faces of the pilgrims seemed to me to wear the ex-
pressions that the little cripple had carved into his stone figures. The old beggars particularly had a look of being fresh
from Aleijadinho's chisel. These seemed deeply sentimental
people. It was easy for them to give way to feeling sorry for
themselves and for others. The twin faucets of sorrow and
joy were right within reach. Their joy in their pilgrimage lay
in the dolefulness of it.

At the foot of the steps the cobbled street was encumbered
by market stalls and flanked by little bars and eating houses.
A quiet jollity reigned. Men and women greeted friends and
neighbors with broad smiles. Children, here as everywhere in
Brazil very much indulged, scuttled about underfoot. In a
smell of cane brandy and sizzling grease and charcoal fires and
spoiled fruit crushed between the cobbles people were enjoy-
ing themselves. Flies zoomed joyously about. Burros and
mules tied to the walls were being fed small swatches of hay.
Radios blared out sambas. From inside a doorway came the
sound of a guitar. In spite of a good deal of filth and ragged
poverty, there was a sense of wellbeing, of a sort of wellinten-
tioned innocence about the people of the back country. I
don't know how much the pilgrims looked at Aleijadinho's
sculptures, or what they thought of them if they did, but it

was obvious that the little cripple was their man: it was their feelings he had carved so painfully into the stone.

Ouro Prêto the ancient capital of the province of Minas Gerais was quite different. There the colonial baroque took on a stately and imperial air. It was a city of long façades and irregularshaped squares with stony mountains at the end of every vista. Though sprung from a different goldrush and from a different culture, and artfully built of carved stone and stucco instead of being knocked together out of pine boards, Ouro Prêto had the mining town look as unmistakably as a place like Virginia City in our Sierras. Now it is a city of schools and museums. Students from the mining college give life to the streets. We found Niemeyer's new hotel magnificently unfinished. Chill mountain airs romped through the corridors. The covers were scanty and the beds were of unforgettable hardness.

On the way back the Whites and I spent a cosy night in a nineteenth century sort of family hotel in a textile town called Juiz de Fora, which means something like "the law west of the Pecos"; and then returned over the rainy mountains of the coastal range to the cosmopolitan comforts of Copacabana. We had become fast friends. We couldn't quite imagine why we had been having such a good time.

Sespe: An Alliance That Worked

My next expedition was to the Rio Doce.

When a British company built the Rio Doce Railroad to bring out the iron ore from the stripmine at Itabira in the high mountains of Minas Gerais, its construction vied as a mankiller with the Madeira-Mamoré Railroad in the far western reaches of Amazonas, which was said to have cost a life for every tie that was laid. Now the Special Public Health Service, organized with the help of the Rockefeller Foundation, in the good neighbor days of World War II, had turned the valley into a health resort, so the story went. I arranged to go see.

It was a rough trip. Almost anywhere else in the world the trip might have seemed uncomfortably rough, but the good humor of my companions and the general tendency to take things as they came, turned it into a pleasant outing.

In those days no matter where you were going from Rio you arrived at Santos Dumont airport before dawn and stood around drinking coffee while the plane crews collected and prepared in their leisurely Brazilian way for the takeoff. Dr. Penido, who was at that time in charge of the Rio Doce Health Service, turned up just in time to insist on paying for my coffee. A complete stranger got ahead of me with a coin when I tried to buy a newspaper. Our first stop on the flight north was in a scorched meadow near a sunflattened little town with redtiled roofs under coconut palms. The passengers piled out on the runway to stretch their legs and clustered round an old man selling green coconuts with straws stuck in to drink the water from. By the time I'd fished some money out of my pocket to pay for my coconut, the steward had already settled for it. *Muito obrigado.* A little embarrassing, this Brazilian hospitality, but it does make a foreigner feel they are glad to have him there.

Vitória, the capital of the State of Espírito Santo and the shipping port for the Itabira ore, turned out to be on the flank of a rocky island. First thing we were all bunched up for a photograph on the terrace of a clubhouse built on the ruins of the fort which used to guard the harbor's narrow mouth. More Public Health Service doctors and a couple of Americans who worked for the Rio Doce Railroad had met us at the airstrip. Now we were confronted with the salutations of the local newspaper editor and of a group of townspeople.

It was Sunday and the sun was bright and the bay was blue and the men wore shining white suits. Inside the clubhouse young people were dancing the samba. While his photographer was crouching and peering the newspaper editor pointed out to me some old prostrate cannon rusting on the ledge below the clubhouse terrace. In the seventeenth century, he said, the Dutch had tried to take Vitória and the defenders had stretched cables from this fort to the granite shore opposite and had sunk a Dutch man-of-war and saved the city for Brazil. It was in this war against the Dutch that Brazilian nationality first came into being. His chest puffed out and he strutted like a bantam as he turned to mug the camera.

The sun was hot and the breeze off the sea was cool. After the shutter clicked, we stood a moment looking out, over the dancing blue waves of the harbor hemmed in by hills, at the redtiled roofs of the brick and stucco town and the small freighters tied up to the wharves and the yellow bulk of the oredocks opposite. There were gulls. A few dark man-of-war birds skimmed overhead.

Was this the mouth of the Rio Doce? I asked. Good Lord no, the mouth of the Rio Doce was miles away to the north. Vitória was the port for the Rio Doce Railroad down from the mines which has to climb out of the valley over a mountain range to get to it. The Rio Doce emptied into a shallow delta and had no decent harbor at its mouth. Everybody began to explain at once that the historical impediment to development in southern and central Brazil had from colonial days been that you always had to climb a mountain range to get into the interior. The iron ore deposits up in the central part of Minas Gerais had been known and worked since the beginning of Brazil, but it was only now that large scale shipment was in sight. In the early days hostile Indians blocked the use of the waterlevel route up the Rio Doce into the mining country. Then it had been malaria . . . "But the main impediment is bureaucracy," one of the engineers interrupted as we climbed into the car to go into town to lunch, "Brazilian bureaucracy."

Brazilian bureaucracy, someone explained from the back seat, was a little special because of the horror of productive work of the literate Brazilian. One of the evils of the Portuguese heritage. No use fussing now about the historical causes but the fact remained that the sort of people who were brought up to become public servants had no practical knowledge of any of the processes of production. The old habit of wearing a long fingernail on the little finger had been the symbol of the educated class that had never done any physical work and never intended to do any. So the Brazilian bureaucrats' notions of production were purely theoretical. This was true more or less of all Latin countries. In Brazil a certain social democracy did occasionally narrow the gulf between the illiterate barefoot producer and the man at the office desk, but it was wide all the same. In the States we suffered from bureaucracy too, but the man at the desk had maybe worked as a section hand on the railroad summers when he was in school, or at least he went home and stoked his own furnace and mowed his own lawn. In most of South America you came out of school belonging to a different race from the man who hoed your garden.

By that time we had arrived at the already shabby modern-style building where the Special Public Health Services, known to everybody as Sespe, had central offices for the Rio Doce region.

Going up in the elevator Dr. Penido explained sadly, in his low rather singsong tones, about the building. It had been built as a hospital. A modern hospital was very much needed in Vitória, but the money had run out and all that had come of it had been a small private clinic on the lower floor. The rest was rented out for offices. That was the sort of thing his service was determined to avoid. Sespe never entered into a project unless the funds were on hand not only to complete it but to maintain it.

Did I know the history of Sespe? I nodded.

I had spent some time in the main office in Rio where I had found the same low tones, the same frankness and modesty, talking to Dr. Candou, then its Brazilian chief, and Dr. Cambell, who represented the State Department's Institute of Inter-American Affairs.

Although Brazil had a public health service back in the fifties of the last century, before the United States in fact, that service fell into bureaucratic lethargy, along with many other useful organizations set up by Pedro II's imperial administration, under the republican spoils system. There was a revival under Oswaldo Cruz, the Brazilian Walter Reed; but the new generation of Brazilian public health doctors got their training during the worldwide battle of the Rockefeller Foundation against yellow fever, and in the war of extermination against the *gambiae* mosquito in the eastern bulge during the period of the Second World War. Before DDT they used arsenic and pyrethrum. These campaigns resulted in the only cases known to medical history of the complete eradication of a species. The *Aedes* mosquito which carried yellow fever was eliminated in Brazil, and the *gambiae* which carried pernicious malaria.

Then in 1942 in the early days of Franklin Roosevelt's Good Neighbor policy, Major General George C. Dunham, the author of a famous textbook on public health, was sent down from Washington to help Latin America set up a health program. He had experience in the Philippines in inducing local governing bodies to come in on public health programs and was convinced that a health organization to be effective had to be based on the cooperation of the people themselves. That was the genesis of the Sespe idea. Most of the Brazilian staff obtained their practical education in the field under the Rockefeller organization and their theoretical training at public health centers in the States.

We were standing in the empty office looking at a map of the valley tacked up on the wall with glassheaded pins in various colors indicating the different services.

"To produce an island of public health in each place we work," said Dr. Penido, "first we have to build privies for the people. You see we start from zero in this country. Then we give them pure water."

Monty Montanare pricked up his ears at that. Monty was a lanky young American engineer with a long North Italian nose, a graduate of the Seabees in the Aleutians and on Guam. Building water systems was his business. "Don't touch the water in Vitória" he admonished me gruffly. "Once we get in the valley you can drink all you want."

Monty seemed to be executive director of the expedition. After a glance at his wrist watch he announced it was time to eat; he'd ordered the linecar for three. After a tremendous Brazilian luncheon, which started with salad and coldcuts, and proceeded through steak and rice and chicken and beans to culminate in roast pork smothered in fried eggs, Monty shepherded us into two automobiles and we were driven across the iron bridge to the railroad station on the mainland.

The linecar of course hadn't arrived yet, though it was after three, so we roamed around looking at the old wood-burning locomotives with their funnelshaped stacks, like the locomotives in prints by Currier and Ives, that were shunting the cars in the freightyard, and at the great piles of wood along the tracks. I wondered how many manhours of work it took to cut all that wood up in the hills and to bring it down by oxcart or on the backs of burros or of men to the railroad.

At a church on the shore a ringing of bells had started. The steamboats at the docks across the harbor were blowing their whistles. Down the middle of the stream in the sparkling sunlight came a long string of launches and rowboats decorated with green and yellow streamers. From the shore came cheers and the popping of rockets. *Foguetes* are part of the Portuguese heritage. It was from China, probably, the early navigators brought home a taste for fireworks. Somewhere a brass band was playing. It was the procession of some saint being carried by water from one shrine to another. Before we had time to find out the name of the saint the linecar had backed in beside the platform.

It was a big green stationwagon sort of vehicle mounted on railroad trucks and driven by a diesel engine. We had to hurry to get off in order to meet the passenger train coming down the singletrack line at the proper siding. First we circled the conical mountain on the track the oretrains used. We stopped over the oredocks. Walter Runge, another American, who worked for the company that was repairing the line, stepped out and picked up a piece of heavy blue and red rock.

"Sixtyeight per cent," he said. "Just about the richest iron ore in the world. The railroad's still sketchy. It comes a long way, and it takes a long time, but it gets here. These oredocks could have been better designed but the ships somehow get loaded. There were times when we wondered if they ever would."

At the edge of the yards the bucktoothed mulatto driver had to stop the car suddenly to send his black assistant running back to the station to get his orders. The railroad was operated on the old English block system; only one piece of equipment allowed at a time in a block. At last the boy arrived panting with a green slip in his hand and we went off rattling and lurching over the newlaid rails, past bamboo fences and small thatched huts with mud floors and yards planted with scrawny papayas where a few skinny chickens pecked about and dirty children black and brown and grayish white, naked or dressed in rags that barely covered them, rolled and played in the thick dust.

One set of houses, freshly built for railroad workers, stood out along the track neat and white with scrubbed tiled floors.

Immediately the town fell away and we were crossing sun-seared savannas that had once been planted in sugarcane and where occasionally the ruins of a stone and adobe fazenda crumbled under a bristling mat of vegetation. The abolition of slavery had made them uneconomical.

Scattered white and gray zebu cattle with big humps grazed on the plain. The railroad swept into bare rocky hills. The hills were scorched and smoldering because this was the season when they burned over the land to plant it when the rains began.

In the valleys there was an occasional ranch house with mud walls and tiled roofs set in a bunch of tattered banana trees As the evening began to thicken in smoke and dusk the line wound in endless curves up a rocky valley. In the distance blue humped mountains rose from dark rock faces into fantastic cones against the sky.

Walter Runge was a hefty young man from New Jersey who had studied his engineering at Rutgers. He pointed out with a craftsman's pride the work his outfit had done, straightening curves, eliminating grades, laying new rails, reballasting. He made you feel that this rickety singletrack line into the wilderness was an amusing and capricious toy to be coddled and petted and gradually babied out of its errors and vices.

Night came down on us suddenly. As the car came to a stop on a siding he pointed up into a barely visible tangle of matted trees. "We had a camp up there . . . All over here is swamps . . . The place is full of wonderful orchids . . . Before DDT we had to keep a double payroll because half the men were always down with malaria."

"Any wild animals?"

"There might be some deer. They claim Espírito Santo is a great place for jaguars but I never saw one . . . Ticks and chiggers keep you so busy you don't worry about other wild life." He started scratching at the very thought of them.

We were waiting for an oretrain to come down. The night was dead silent. A few grasshoppers made a rasping noise in the trees. From away up the line we heard the whistle of the engine and the rattle of the trucks of the orecars coming round the curves.

The doctors were talking about jungle yellow fever that had been found to be carried by the *Haemagogus* mosquitoes that bred in the little pools of water in the forks of high forest trees. Now that the standard type had been eliminated, the jungle type was the next enemy to be vanquished. People called it the bridegroom's disease because it was often contracted by young men who went out to clear themselves a piece of land when they married. The yellow fever inspectors kept track of it by watching for the bodies of the little animals that lived in the highest level of the rainforest. If they found a lot of dead monkeys it meant that there was yellow fever about.

The oretrain went slambanging past. After that the line was clear. We crossed the divide and went lurching and jangling through the night round long curves over singing rails until we roared with siren hooting into the main street of a place called Colatina.

There were creamcolored stucco housefronts and stores and cafés lit up theatrically by a string of electric lights.

The local doctors had come to meet us at the station. *Abraços* and *felicidades*. We walked to the hotel beside flatcars piled with immense logs of *peroba* wood. Now this hotel, Dr. Penido was explaining, was an example of how public health worked. I should have seen it a year ago. Now at least the kitchen was clean and the bedrooms and the dining room and bar. I'd be distressed by the toilet but he was working on that. Gradually. Gradually . . . Keeping a toilet clean was the result of years of education. In the Rio Doce Valley a privy was a monstrous novelty five years ago.

Next morning we were out early walking round the town. Rosy mist hung low over the broad sluggish puttycolored river. The bridge had been built for a railroad that never got completed; battered trucks were coming across it into town and occasionally a cart with whining wheels of solid planking drawn by a majestic pair of humped zebu oxen.

We walked down the cobbled street toward the Health Center. On the way Dr. Penido and Dr. Lavigne, the local chief of public health operations, proudly showed off the market. No rotting piles of garbage as in Rio. The stalls were clean. The vegetables looked freshwashed. The butchershop was screened and the marble tables had just been scrubbed. To be sure somebody had left open the little window in the screen through which the sales were made. Dr. Penido noted the fact philosophically. The next time it would be closed. "Education," he said in a tone of infinite patience.

The Health Center had an air of quiet gaiety about it. It was an airy little building of gray stone and white stucco, designed I was told by Peter Pfister in the States, with a cool covered patio between the two rows of offices and consulting rooms, where people could wait out of the sun and in the breeze. At one end there was a playground for children. You could see that people enjoyed coming here. Varicolored children were scrambling around on swings and seesaws. People had brought their dogs.

In back was a sample vegetable garden with vigorous rows of lettuce, beets, dill, chicory, carrots, turnips, magnificent tomatoes. Dr. Penido explained that the people of the Rio Doce Valley had forgotten about growing vegetables. Beans and rice and occasionally a small gourd named *chu-chú* cooked with a strip of sundried beef constituted the daily diet, sprinkled plentifully with dry manioc flour so that you could make the mess into a ball with your fingers and shove it into your mouth. Now, in the town at least, the Public Health Service was cultivating a taste for vegetables among the people. If somebody proved that he could raise a garden he was given free seeds. Education.

The doctors tried to get the schoolchildren into health clubs so that they would interest their parents in sanitation and a wellbalanced diet. If they educated the children, the children would educate their parents. The trouble was that not all the children went to school and, of those who did, the great majority dropped out after the first three years.

In the offices they showed me their filing system. A simple and usable filing system was the crux of the problem. To produce an island of public health where there had been not the faintest notion of it before, you had to keep a record. That was the best thing the Americans had taught them, the Brazilian doctors agreed; a method of keeping a simple and adequate record without bureaucratic clogging. There were cards for every family in town showing its health record and the results of the visits of the district nurse. There were cards for individual patients. There were cards for every butcher-shop, bakery, bar, restaurant, hotel and boarding house, showing its sanitary record, recommendations made, improvements if any.

"Always," said Dr. Penido in his quiet drawling voice, "we try to use persuasion . . . We try to get people to feel they want to improve things themselves. Then when they feel the benefit they become interested."

As we walked out we passed a row of humble beatenlooking women waiting in line to get free boiled milk or made up formulas for their babies. Some of them had shoes but many of them hadn't. Their skimpy dresses were none too clean.

"Five years ago," said Dr. Penido in his low voice, smiling his sad disdainful smile, "they were drinking polluted water out of the river and depositing their excrement in the bushes . . . We can isolate the lepers. We can cure yaws with about ninety cruzeiros' worth of penicillin, we can cure hookworm . . . DDT has malaria on the run. We can vaccinate for diphtheria and smallpox but to have really universal public health in this country we have to produce models that people will copy . . . sanitary islands."

As he went out into the street a dark look came over his face, as if somebody had said something that had hurt his feelings. "Now we face tuberculosis," he said solemnly. It seemed as if TB increased with civilization. When people lived in huts in the crannies of the mountains they didn't have so much TB. "As we clean up other diseases TB seems to spread."

Across the street from the Health Center was a very much larger building ornamented with a great deal of carved stone in pompous Manueline style.

"What is that building?" I asked.

Dr. Penido had walked on scowling up the street. Somebody else answered the question. That was the lying-in hospital built by the state of Espírito Santo some years ago. A fine building but the trouble was it never opened. Funds ran out . . . Another Brazilian project.

We walked back to the station down the main street between stucco walls that glowed in the failing sunlight. At one corner in front of a drygoods store stood a sallow man of middle age with the respectable paunch of a father of a family. All he wore was a fake Indian feather girdle and a feather headdress. He carried a bow and arrow in his hand. Now and then he emitted hoarse fake Indian noises and made wardance steps inside of the drygoods box he stood in. As we passed we noticed that he was barefooted and that the box was full of broken glass. It was some wily Syrian's idea of how to advertise his cotton prints.

The Triumph of the Oldtime Privy

The valley was murky and hot that morning. Brush fires burned on the mountains on either side. Clearing land for new coffee plantations. The ranks of shrubby shinyleaved dark-green trees I'd been looking at in the hollows of the hills were coffee, the doctors said. In the lower part of the valley the planters were doing very well with cacao; up here it was all coffee. New plantings. Many of the trees were just about to come into bearing. In a few years the Rio Doce would be a great coffeeproducing region . . . if the world market didn't glut with coffee. "Brazil is the land of the future," one of them broke in bitterly.

The linecar jerked and jounced over the rails. At every station teams of zebu oxen, four, five, and six yokes pulling in line, were hauling up the logs of peroba wood from the water's edge. They strained forward in slow unison in a swirl of red dust. Alongside ran barefoot men and boys the color of the dust steering the oxen with shouts and groans and the touch of their long slender wands.

The river wound broad and sullen under a glaze of heat between rocky islets. Now and then we waited on a siding for a long oretrain to grind heavily past.

We were out of the malaria belt. The chief enemy of man in this upper part of the valley was a clever little fluke known as a *schistosoma* that spent part of its lifecycle in a watersnail. From out of the watersnail came millions of microscopic wormlike creatures that joyfully sought out the feet of a man wading or the hands of a woman washing and made their way through the pores into the blood stream where they hatched out eggs and produced a highly disagreeable disease known as schistosomiasis. The preventive measure was oldfashioned privies. The way the schistosoma got back into the streams and ponds to infect the snails was through the human feces.

"In Aimorés we'll show you the snails . . . On my way back from the States I stopped off in Venezuela where they are making progress in poisoning the snails. We are experimenting with that method, but meanwhile," said Dr. Penido with his ironical smile, "the answer seems to be privies. Here I spent twelve years of my life studying medicine, in Brazil and in the United States" he exclaimed in a tone of mock deprecation, "and I spend my time building privies."

In the freight yard at Aimorés we found the health service's sleeping and laboratory car. The sleeper was in charge of a shrewdlooking brown steward named Joaquim. Joaquim had some sort of a rising on his chin which was swathed in an immense wad of bandages and adhesive tape like the false beard of a pharaoh. He served us lunch in the tiny dining section of the car. Dr. Penido announced, laughing his soft sarcastic laugh, that it was just as well the car was there because the Aimorés hotel had turned out so hopelessly unsanitary that he had induced the owner to pull it down entirely and start all over from scratch.

In spite of the loss of its hotel Aimorés was a busy little town full of dusty traffic and new building. House building offers few problems in these parts. A carpenter makes around twenty cents an hour. The valley is full of sawmills and every tiny hamlet has a brick kiln. Everybody complains of the expense and scarcity of cement but they have an abundance of cheap tile and brick. On every street we saw new brick houses going up with tiled roofs, and wellfinished woodwork and beautifully laid parquet floors. From the top of the hill we climbed to visit Monty's waterworks, about half the roofs of the town straggling out over the valleyfloor beneath us looked new. Right at our feet were the new tiny shacks, some of brick and some of the common mud and wooden frame construction, of the workingpeople's suburb which in Brazil is known as a *favela*.

This favela was the best we had seen on the trip. The

houses were in row and each had a yard and a solidly built brick privy. "Look at all the privies," Dr. Penido burst out waving his arms with humorous pride, "An orgy of privies."

"This is such decent housing," said Monty, "we shouldn't call it a favela."

The Favela: Symbol of the New Brazil?

The word favela as usual set off an argument. Everybody started talking at once.

Favela in Brazilian Portuguese means slum. A favela is a particular type of recent slum that takes its name from the hill near Rio where the first one appeared. The favela is the sign and symbol of the population explosion which has resulted from the success of just the sort of public health measures Dr. Penido and his associates were showing off with such pride.

With the growth of industry, and the caving in of the scanty rural economy, people came crowding out of the back country into cities and towns. In the back country they had lived a barefoot life as ungarnished in every aspect as the little huts with dirt floors they were born in and dwelt in and died in, but at least they had space about them and air to breathe. Except in very bad droughts the rural economy had furnished sufficient food. People lived according to certain standards of civilized rustic behavior. The landowner was feudal lord. Feudalism, when it works, is far from being the worst form of human organization.

In the cities the immigrants find no housing ready for them, so they pick themselves out a back lot and put themselves up a shack out of whatever materials are cheapest and handiest just the way they would back up in the hills. Individual initiative. They cook on charcoal. They can't read and write so they don't need much artificial light. The women and children fetch water in gasoline tins from the nearest pump that may be a mile away, just as they would have gone down to the river back home, and they deposit their excrement behind the fence and throw their garbage out on the path just as they always did. The shacks agglomerate into rattletrap settlements, like the Hoovervilles of depression times in the States.

In Rio—this was in 1948—there were said to be three hundred thousand people living in favelas. Today there are nearer a million. You come on favelas in the most unexpected places. In Copacabana a few minutes walk from the hotels and the splendid white apartment houses and the wellkept magnificent beaches you find a whole hillside of favelas overlooking the lake and the Jockey Club. In the center of Rio a few steps from the Avenida Rio Branco on the hill back of one of the most fashionable churches you come suddenly into a tropical jungletown.

In Rio under the pressure of metropolitan life the favelas are even producing a culture of their own. Their religion is one of the many forms of West African voodoo that have taken root in American soil, known there as *macumba*. The artistic and social center is the samba school. The favelas are the spawning ground for Brazil's abundant popular music. I was told of a wealthy songwriter who refused to move out of his favela. How could he? That's where his music came from. If a foreigner turns up on a visit the inhabitants tend to cluster around to show off their favela's best points. Some of the shacks are well built and prettily painted. The views are magnificent. Their owners take pride in their dwellings and fight like tigers to retain possession of them. The main trouble is the lack of water and light. There is no garbage disposal, no sewerage. The police don't dare penetrate; but at that you are probably safer in a Rio favela than in Central park in New York or on a side street in Washington, D.C.

Remembering the smell of dried excrement that haunted the favelas of Rio I could understand the real enthusiasm under Dr. Penido's kidding manner when he stood looking down with the air of a conqueror from the hill at Aimorés, and spoke of islands of public health. I got the feeling that there was more than sanitation at stake, there was the budding of a civilization.

The Rio Doce Valley was no health resort, at least not yet, but I was beginning to feel the excitement of combat, taking part, if only for a few days, in this battle for public health. The diseases had become as personal as people to these doctors. Tagging around with them in the humorous give and take of rough frontier travel, I had begun to feel as they felt, the hostility that lurked in forest pools and in the garbage thrown out back of the hut by a careless housewife, and to exult with them in every puff of vaporized DDT into a damp corner, or in every quinine injection or atabrin pill that was helping drive back the enemy beyond the blue hills that hemmed the valley.

While we wrangled over the sociology of the favelas, Monty was waiting with some impatience to show us his waterstation. The water was pumped up from the river by diesel pumps so that they wouldn't depend on the light and power system which so often broke down. It passed through filters and chemical purifiers. Better water than many towns had in the States, Monty insisted proudly. Inside, the walls were fresh painted and the machinery looked well tended and the tiled floors were sparkling clean. "There's capacity for twice the size of the town," Monty insisted, "up to fifteen thousand people."

A man was on his hands and knees mopping the tiles as we walked through. I looked at him twice because he was white-skinned and had tow hair. His face was lined and haggard and dirty. It's a shock to a northerner in this Rio Doce Valley to find the blond offspring of German or Polish settlers living in the same ragged barefoot dirt as the darkerskinned inhabitants.

"You see," Monty was explaining enthusiastically as he ushered us out on the terrace, "we're all set except for pouring a little more concrete. Then only the cleaning up and landscaping left to do."

I asked who the blond man was. He was not interested. "I dunno. He must be a German. I guess they just hire him for odd jobs."

We stood a while on the terrace to look down into the valley. The sun was setting red into the murk behind a scraggly line of ravaged forest on the crest of a cutover hill. Touched with sultry copper glints the Rio Doce meandered with a distant hiss of broken water among rocks and scrubby islands. It looked a little like the Susquehanna below Harrisburg. An oddlooking black bird with brown markings like a butterfly was fluttering about a clump of cactus.

Down the path from the waterstation to the favela, naked except for a ragged pair of shorts, with a beaten droop to his shoulders, the blond man went stumbling wearily. He never turned his head to look at us. Holding onto his hand was a little towhaired boy three or four years old who was dressed in short pants and a little striped sweater, a sort of grimy replica of what a little boy of his age would be wearing in some distant northern home. Looking after them I was remembering what a geographer friend had told me in Rio: "Brazil is the greatest experiment in the settling of European man in the tropics, but that doesn't mean it is always successful."

Islands of Public Health

Above Aimorés next day the valley was narrower and dustier and drier. Fires burned more fiercely in the hills. A streaky ceiling of smoke and dust hung over the river. On steep eroding pastures, which were a network of dry cowpaths, big zebu cattle grazed in herds. Gangs were working on the line. Occasionally we had to stop while the section gang ahead lowered a new length of track into place. The settlements had a raw backwoods look.

At the little stations where the linecar had to wait for the oretrains coming down, there was a great deal going on. There were ferries on the river, flatboats, that traveled on a cable, ingeniously propelled by the force of the current. A shriek of mechanical saws came from the sawmills. Carts were bringing in cut firewood for the railroad or bags of charcoal to be shipped to the charcoalburning iron furnaces up the valley. At every siding the oxteams were churning the dust as they dragged the trunks of peroba trees up from the water's edge. At a place called Conselheiro Pena three men were maneuvering the great logs up onto a platform with a team of eleven yokes of zebu oxen, and rolling them onto flatcars. Their only tool was the slender poles they used to handle the oxen.

At a place called Timiritinga, which, so the station master proudly explained, had just changed its name from Tarumirím, there was a long wait for the daily passenger train down from Valadares. Monty and I roamed through the ankledeep dust between the two rows of forlorn low houses of plastered adobe, looking at the pigs and the scattered garbage and the open square of sunscorched weeds that was laid out for the *praça* to be.

"You see," Monty was saying dreamily, "this work can be expanded indefinitely. We are just in the shape now where we know how to do things . . . We've had five years to make our mistakes and to work up a system. We've got the blueprint and all we need to do now is expand it. At first it was all by guess and by God as they used to say in the Navy . . . When my contract expired I went back home and intended to stay but I got to thinking that this work was about as important as a man could find to do and I said to my wife could she stick it . . . with the baby and everything . . . and she said she guessed she could . . . so back we came. And now when we're all rearing to go down here and Brazilian organizations are really interested in putting up money for more public health work, it looks as if the American end was petering out, as if there wasn't much interest in Washington. The folks back home are forgetting about Brazil."

We went into a little bar to get one of the tiny cups of strong black coffee that are sprinkled through every Brazilian day. An incredibly tattered young white woman with her hair in a ratsnest and her breasts blobbing out of her grimy dress brought us our coffee. There was a tobaccocolored man with a felt hat and a mustache sitting at the only other table. Right away he told us that Timiritinga had not only changed its name but it had just this day been created a city. Now there would be money to appropriate for public health.

We heard the siren blow from the linecar. That meant that the driver had his orders to proceed. Swallowing the scalding thimbleful of coffee we hurried over to the station. Our friend with the mustache followed us all the way to the linecar explaining how much the people of the new founded city of Timiritinga wanted Sespe to help them with their sanitation. "You see," Monty nudged me excitedly as we settled back in our seats, "you see, it's like that all over."

The Lost Leader

My trip up the railroad ended at a raw new town named Governador Valadares. You could see the outlines of a future city plan scratched out in the red clay among the stumps and carcasses of the felled forest trees. Eight thousand people lived in a straggle of shanties among sawmills and brick kilns. The town lay on a bend of the Rio Doce opposite a great battlemented mountain with a smooth granite face that soared out of sight through the level layers of smoke and mist that roofed in the valley.

In the crowded freightyards beyond the station we found Joaquim waiting for us with his sleeper, which had come up on the passenger train. The car was still oven hot from the day's sun, and airless because every space between the tracks was piled high with cut wood for the locomotives, but the narrow showerbath where a trickle of tepid water washed off the grimed red dust of the valley was a delight.

All the way up Dr. Penido had been promising us a good restaurant in Valadares so after everybody had bathed we straggled off along the broad main street already planted with trees, up past a new circular park at the intersection of the main streets still in the excavation stage, to a café presided over by a huge lightbrown man in a cook's hat and apron whom the doctors explained had worked as a tailor until it had occurred to him that he'd rather be a cook. And a very good cook he turned out to be.

After a great deal of steak and rice washed down by Portuguese wine to the tune of that most ingratiating Brazilian toast: "*As nossas boas qualidades que não são poucas* [To our good qualities, which are not few]"—we sat a long time talking and smoking. The Brazilians were trying to explain to the Americans, still in a gentle friendly way, that they felt let down, after all the propaganda of the Good Neighbor policy and wartime cooperation, by the lack of interest the American people now showed in their problems.

"But you don't want American capital. You want to develop your own oil industry and your own iron and steel."

"*O petróleo é nosso.* That's mostly propaganda," said one of the doctors laughing.

"But everybody believes in it. The papers in Rio are full of it."

"We don't want American imperialism but we do want American interest and help, especially technical help . . . and dollars. We'd like more help for public health."

"Perhaps what hurts us," said Dr. Penido in his gentle

ironical tone, "is a certain lack of comprehension . . . I feel it myself with Americans, not with all but with some even at this table." It seemed to me he looked rather hard at Monty. Monty looked glum. "I was two years studying public health at Johns Hopkins . . . Baltimore is a very nice city. I had a very good time there, met many damn splendid guys, but I felt a certain lack of comprehension."

He went on to talk in a dreamy voice about European culture. He had lived in Paris as a child. As he talked I could see him, short pants and bare knees, playing in the Parc Monceau. The loss of Paris was something no Brazilian could get over, the loss of that feeling of being linked to the evolving traditions of European civilization: the Greeks, the Romans, the Arabs, the French, link by link, through the ages. The war had blacked out Europe and Brazilians missed that stimulus. The North Americans didn't have it. It was hard to put your finger on it. It was something that made a man feel part of civilization. Perhaps that was why they were disappointed in the United States.

The town lights had gone out. Our immense host brought in an oil lamp and set it on the big Electrolux refrigerator behind the table.

"There have been a series of disappointments," one of the other doctors burst out. "After the victory we thought that America would assume a world leadership like the Europe our fathers remembered."

"Without imperialism? How can you do it?"

There was a polite shrugging of shoulders.

"America seems so much weaker in victory," sighed Dr. Penido. "But," he banged his fist on the table and went on briskly, "the important thing is that we have produced a successful experiment in international cooperation . . . Sespe would not exist without the cooperation of both Americans and Brazilians. We have proved that it works. We have learned a method. Now we could go on to do great things, if just at this crucial moment in the United States you did not seem to lose interest."

"We feel," one of the others echoed, "a certain lack of comprehension."

Dr. Penido yawned and rose to his feet. It was late. We groped our way through unlit streets and freightyards stacked with corded wood back to our sleeping car.

The Rockcrusher That Never Gets Out of Order

In the morning a small plane came down from the mine at Itabira to pick me up. Now I was going to see where all those orecars came from. As the pilot spiraled up from the airstrip at Valadares to vault the first range of razorbacked mountains I began to note the extent of the devastation of the country. As far as I could see into the murk fires made a red marbling on the cutover slopes. The mountains under us smoldered like burnt papers in a grate.

Pastures along the winding streams showed that fine network of cattlepaths that comes from overgrazing. Houses, usually solitary on a hillock in a valley, were scarce. Near a house you could usually make out the broad bunched leaves of a few banana trees and some tiny green squares of cultivated land. It was hard to imagine how such a sparse population could so ravage the hills. The railroad's demands for firewood, the burning of charcoal to cook with, and its use in iron furnaces, had already gutted the forests for an enormous tract of country. The logging out of lumber for export did the rest. As we climbed again to clear a new set of granite escarpments the valleys below were drowned in smoke. The plane tore into speeding clouds that packed tight like cotton wool against the windows.

There was no ceiling at all over the airfield at the mine, so we had to turn back. When we landed at Valadares again the Brazilian business man who shared the seat with me shouted in my ear. "I was anxious," he said, "until the pilot told me he was the father of eight. The father of eight just has to be careful."

As we walked with throbbing ears across the field to the shelter, he added that he wondered whether as a foreigner I understood the significance of what I was seeing in the Vale do Rio Doce: "It is climbing a series of steps. First the valley was so unhealthy we could hardly keep up the railroad. The malaria service and public health make sanitary the valley so that we can improve the railroad . . . America helps Brazil up a step. In the State of Minas Gerais we have the richest iron deposit in the world but to get it out we had only picks and shovels. The American loan buys the machinery to work it . . . Another step . . ."

"But what about the campaign against American imperialism?"

"That," he said, "is the labor of Communists."

He put his arm around my shoulder and offered to buy my lunch. After lunch, which, since the public health doctors were still in Valadares, turned out to be a second farewell celebration, the father of eight did manage to land us on the wet hilltop airstrip at Itabira. The mountains all around were still draped in clouds. The drenched air made us shiver after the heat of the valley.

The quiet man in khaki who came out to meet us introduced himself as Gil Whitehead, American manager of the mine for the Rio Doce Company. "It's too bad that you can't see the peak of Caué," he said and looked up at the murky ceiling just overhead. "I'd like you to see the magic mountain."

While we waited for the clouds to lift we drove round the old town that climbed up steep red ridges to a suburb of neat new houses for the skilled workmen and to the big concrete hangar which could house the new machine shops. The valleys below were full of tattered mist. The weather had settled down to a cold drizzle. The hunks of wet ore shone as they thundered down the chutes into the orecars.

Gil Whitehead had a selfeffacing manner and a slow drawl. Now and then his smoldering sort of humor would let out a sudden flash. He explained how production had increased and how, with the improvement of the railroad, production would increase still more. For Brazil the iron ore, which was going to steel mills in the United States and Canada, where they used it instead of scrap, would mean essential dollars in the world market. And when the new rockcrushing machinery came production would really spurt.

"Meanwhile," he said and pointed to a little brown man with a hammer trudging up the road in the rain, "we are using the only rockcrusher that, in these parts, never gets out of order."

He glanced out of the window. The rain had stopped but the clouds hung lower than ever. "Let's go on up anyway." He drove me up the broad zigzag road that vanished into a ceiling of cloud. "You've heard them speak of metaling a road," he said. "Well this road is sixty per cent pure iron."

When we stepped out of the car the driven clouds snapped like wet toweling in our faces. He told me I was standing on top of two hundred and fifty million metric tons of hematite. The trouble was it was such a long way to Pittsburgh.

He pointed to a quarrylike face of rock. "Simplest operation in the world. All we have to do is blast it down. Since we started in 1944 we've taken twentythree meters off the top of the peak." My eyes followed the sweep of his hand. Under the glistening rock face men were at work among the piles of ore with little sledgehammers, making small ones out of big ones.

Here and there they lit fires of sticks or broken boards for a little warmth. There were spindling white men and tall broadshouldered Negroes and small compact wiry men in all shades of coffee and copper and bronze. Some wore sandals and some were barefooted. Many had gunnysacks tied around them against the cold. A few had tattered cloaks or mud-caked ponchos. As they worked away their hammers rang on the dense ore.

That was my first sight of the Brazilian working man in the mass, of the longsuffering happygolucky nomadic hordes who spread over the vast extent of the country moving from plantation to mine to lumbermill or construction camp, illnourished, ridden with illness, enduring cold and heat and hunger, tightening their belts, and singing their sambas and breeding children and somehow getting the work done.

The Brazilian West

A few days later, five hundred miles to the west I saw the same people under happier conditions. This was at Ceres, a new agricultural settlement which the great roadbuilder Bernardo Sayão was opening up on the Rio das Almas in the western part of the State of Goiás.

Flying west through the bumpy air over the knotted snarl of the mountains of Minas Gerais there were mighty few towns to look down on and almost no roads. You saw below you a lioncolored landscape of burnedover slopes with green strips of cultivated land spreading up the river bottoms. Rarely a tiny house shone white as sugar in the slanting morning light. The hills were a tangle of wandering mule and cattle tracks. Men and animals had walked there for centuries.

This infinity of wandering tracks testified to the still nomadic life of the backlands. A man and his family would live in some cabin in the hills until the land they worked was worn out and then they would have to pull up stakes and walk, with their few possessions on their heads, for hundreds of miles to find some patch of virgin brush which they could burn over for a new plantation. They burned the larger trees for charcoal. The first few years the scorched forest loam gave them good crops, but the winds blew it off and the rains washed it away and the crops ate it up and after a while they had to move on again.

The copilot, a dapper young man from Rio who spoke very good English, came back into the cabin to explain that the state of Minas was one of the oldest settled sections of Brazil, a little stagnant now, but—he spread out his arms—with an immense future. Far to the north on the indigosmudged horizon, he pointed out the clouds that hid Caué, the iron mountain. I told him I had just come from there. "Before it was gold," he shouted excitedly, putting his lips against my ear. "Now it is iron . . . The iron deposits stretch across the state of Minas in the shape of a gigantic dollar sign."

He went back to his place when the plane began to lose altitude over Belo Horizonte, the capital of Minas Gerais. Spiraling down for a landing we had glimpses of the regular avenues lined with trees and the tall white buildings of the city which was started fifty years ago on a plan based on L'Enfant's plan for Washington.

Nearer the airfield shone the angular constructions of glass and concrete designed by Niemeyer and some other pupils of Le Corbusier's for a suburban development round the lake of Pampulha. Among these buildings at Pampulha are some of Niemeyer's most original and imaginative works. It is odd that a professing Communist should have designed such a pretty church. Unfortunately the project, suffering the fate of so many projects in this land of magniloquent blueprints, received a setback from a most unexpected cause. The lake was discovered to be full of snails infested by the wicked little schistosoma. Until some way is found of killing the parasite or the snail, the development of Pampulha was said to be at a standstill.

After leaving Belo Horizonte we flew west for hours and hours. The few tiny settlements were out of sight of the airfields, which become more and more rudimentary as we advanced into the rolling country, interspersed by great plains, of the then new state of Goiás. After seven hours flight from Rio we were in Goiânia. This new capital of a new state was only fifteen years old. It consisted of an avenue of feathery trees to the governor's palace, some public buildings and a few cross streets of rough stuccoed houses, a new hotel already falling to pieces, and some very nicely printed booklets of plans for the future.

The hotel was a collector's item. This was a time in South America when the more cheerful travelers collected bad hotels as a sort of hobby. I kept thinking of Dr. Penido's reflections about how much education it took to keep a toilet clean. One of the oddities of this particular bathroom was that the doorknob would come off in the hand of the unhappy guest, thereby trapping him in the malodorous precinct. Banging on the door brought no response. The procedure was to escape by climbing over the transom that led into the adjoining kitchen. Busy clouds of flies buzzed back and forth over that transom.

Though pigs still rooted in the muddy streets, Goiânia already boasted a school of music and an academy of letters. I sat in the hotel's tiny bar, drinking excellent cold beer with a couple of congenial members of the Goiânia academy, while waiting for a suitable hour to call on the governor, who had hospitably offered to send me out to the federal agricultural colony the next day on one of his planes. They had brought along some magnificent booklets describing the plans for the new federal capital of Brazil which was to be established on a high plateau about a hundred miles to the north, a plateau that boasted, they told me, a delicious temperate climate, where wheat grows in abundance and where all the plants and animals of the temperate zone, including European man, would flourish.

The development of Brazil has been blocked for three hundred years by the colonial mentality of a people trapped between the mountains and the sea, they said. The way to break loose was to move the center of the nation boldly up into the plateau. Their eyes shone and their chests expanded as they talked.

This must have been, I kept thinking, how our early enthusiasts for the North American West talked and glowed, sitting in some rickety tavern on the site of Washington City, when the subject turned to the Ohio or the great dimly discerned prairies west of the Mississippi.

Before modern sanitation and trucks and airplanes all this was a dream; but now, my hosts kept assuring me, it was possible. The federal capital was written into the constitution. It had to come true. By history and tradition and by its racial admixtures Brazil was the best adapted of all the nations of European stock to conquer the tropics. The first step towards achievement would be moving the federal capital.

When I asked whether there was any way of reaching this marvelous plateau, they said it would be difficult. You had to go by a small plane to a rather uncertain airstrip. From there it was eight hours horseback up to the site. If it rained, it would be hard to get back. Neither of them had ever been.

"But where does the Communist movement fit into all this enterprising talk? Haven't you already got too much bureaucracy?"

The younger of my hosts spoke up.

"At eighteen I was a Communist, like everybody else. We have malaria and jungle fever and a million diseases, but our worst disease is poverty. Young intellectuals feel trammeled at every hand by poverty. We thought communism was a cure for poverty. It seemed to open new careers for young

men of brains. Now I am twentyseven and I have discovered
that communism is just another way of dominating the
masses. Instead of curing poverty it makes poverty universal.
We have got to find other alternatives . . . The Communists
now do not make propaganda for communism. They make
propaganda against . . . against North America . . . against
the rich, against anybody who is successful. In Rio they tell
the poor people living in the favelas: 'We will throw out the
landlords and you shall live in luxury in the hotels and the
apartment houses in Copacabana.' It is simple. It works.
Many of our most intelligent men, particularly poets, artists,
architects are subject to this illusion. They have not thought
the thing through to the end."

"It is up to you North Americans to give us an alternative,"
said the older man. "During the war the speeches of the
great Roosevelt gave us an ideal to fight for. Since he died
the United States seems to be drifting. You seem suddenly
old and reactionary. We read about the Marshall Plan for Europe, but when the Communists tell us it is imperialism we
tend to believe them. All we see here is the scarcity of dollars."

"We Brazilians," the younger man burst out, "are a people
of noble impulses. We hate war and militarism. We believe
in progress. We are a people of grandiose illusions. That is
why the Communist movement here is like your Mr. Wal-
lace's party in the States. It flourishes in the best society.
Many fine people in all walks of life have allowed themselves
to be deceived because no one has offered them a better
plan."

"Then," said the older man, "there is envy in every human
heart. You are rich and we are poor. The Communists play
on the envy of the poor for the rich. The cure is a great movement of expansion that will furnish us with new illusions."

He looked at his watch. His voice suddenly took on the

plush tones of a master of protocol. "It is time to go. His Excellency will be expecting us to make a short call at the palace."

Sayão's Colônia

Next morning the governor's airplane deposits my young literary friend, the local circuit judge, and me on an airstrip which they tell me is almost exactly in the center of Brazil. As the plane takes off again in a drive of dust we feel small and lonely under the enormous sky.

We are standing beside a new gravel road that stretches straight into the dusty distance in either direction. Behind us is the ragged airstrip and in front of us a line of great trees that hides the river, and all around a rolling country of high scrub vegetation shimmering in the heat.

The sun, already high, beats down on us hard as hail so we take cover under the porch of a long hut thatched with palm leaves. Inside we find a counter and some shelves of groceries and a pale sweatylooking heavyset man with a week's growth of stubble on his chin. Immediately we are all drinking *cafezinhos* out of the inevitable tiny white cups.

First thing I ask, "Is Bernardo Sayão at the Colônia Agrícola?"

"He is," says the pale man enthusiastically. Then he explains that we still have three leagues to go. We must be patient. They will have seen the plane and will send out for us from the colônia. Sayão always sends out for people, Sayão attends to everything.

The pale man turns out to be a Russian, from the Ukraine. He has lived twentyone years in Brazil. He made big money in São Paulo as a machinist, but when he heard about the colony and the road into the north he'd moved out here. He steps in back behind a bamboo partition and brings out a diving helmet. Gold, he says, rolling his bloodshot gray eyes;

he dove in the rivers for gold. Was he making money at it? One eye crinkles up like a parrot's and his face takes on that sly look of the peasant on the steppe. He doesn't answer but he holds up his thumb and forefinger and rubs them together vigorously.

Before we know what has happened we are adrift in a tumultuous argument about the Soviet Union. The pale man insists that Russia behaves as she does because she is ringed by treacherous enemies. England and America have always been her enemies. My literary friend from Goiânia brings up the Stalin-Hitler Pact. The Brazilian judge, a small brown sparrowlike man with tortoiseshell glasses, perks up and asks if the Russians did right to partition Poland. In 1918 the imperialist nations fought Russia, the pale man shouts back, fingering his diving helmet in a threatening way as if about to use it for a weapon. We lean across the counter and roar at him.

Meanwhile an audience is gathering, an aged scarecrow with a face of stained leather puckered on one side by some sort of ulcer, a soiled barelegged boy with a cast in his eye, a dog, two hens and a rooster. A pig sticks his snout in through a rent in the bamboo wall. Two tiny yellowfaced children peek in beside him.

We are all sweating like horses. The pale man tears the shirt off his damp chest in an agony of conviction. It is all lies we are telling about the Soviet Union. Then he lays his thick forefinger along his nose and crinkles up his eye with that sly look again and says, "In all this there is a mystery . . . There is a very secret mystery. It is true that there is no liberty now but the secret of Russia is liberty in the future."

"Look here," the judge asks him, "if you are such an admirer of the Soviet Union how is it you've been spending all these years in Brazil looking for gold like a capitalist?"

Suddenly the pale man smiles all over his face. He slaps his wet chest. He has a friend in São Paulo, he drawls, who is a doctor and writes very brilliant articles against alcoholism. This doctor wrote a whole book against alcoholism but whenever his friends meet this doctor he is in a bar buying himself a drink. The pale man thrusts out his hand laughing. He shakes hands all around then he brings out another set of cafezinhos on the house.

The cloud of dust that has been coming towards us down the road turns out to contain a bus, a junglestained paleblue bus bulging with passengers and packages. The bus stops in front of the palmthatched hut. A few grimy passengers straggle out to have themselves a coffee. The bus is on its way to the colônia. We are fitted in among dogs and bundles and crates of fowls and the bus starts off grinding and lurching on its slow way through the shabby dryseason jungle. After a while we begin to pass clearings where huge stumps and the skeletons of felled trees still smolder from the burning over; then thatched shelters, a few half finished houses of brick. In front of the first tileroofed houses we see a wattled cage that someone explains is a wolf trap.

We drive downhill through a broad street of low houses which are mostly stores. A crazy bamboo shack has a sign, CAFÉ CERES. We pass a billiard parlor. We cross a green river on a floating bridge supported on clusters of oil drums lashed together. The Rio das Almas. Everybody points out a small white house on top of a grassy hill. That is where Sayão lives.

We are deposited in front of a set of new brick walls which are marked GRANDE HOTEL CERES. We pick our way past the bricklayers, stepping over planking heaped with fresh mortar, and find that the diningroom and a few small alcoves have been completed. The hotel is open for business. The landlady greets us and briskly straightens up a table for our lunch. She speaks English. She comes from the northern part of Bohemia, she says. Oh yes she'd been in the colônia a long time, almost a year.

The place to wash is outside in the yard, two enameled basins on a soapy board and a gasoline can full of water. The tall unshaven man who is washing his face with a great deal of snorting and sputtering turns out to be a Syrian merchant who sells textiles. Yes business is good, good, good. When we settle down to eat I ask the landlady where Sayão is to be found. She shakes her head. He is a hard man to put your finger on. Never stays in one place. She will send a boy over with a message.

"He is not here. Dr. Sayão has gone to Rio," says a young lighthaired woman, nicely dressed as if for shopping in the city, who walks into the diningroom speaking dogmatic English. She sits down beside us. She comes from Vienna. She has an apartment in Rio. Her husband is a Hungarian. They are settling. If she likes it she will give up her apartment in Rio. If we want to learn about the colônia we must stay many days because it is very interesting. We must come to see her new house. Eventually Dr. Sayão will return.

The rosy young couple who walked in while we were talking turned out to be Swiss. He was an agronomist under contract to the Brazilian Government. Did they know anything about the whereabouts of Dr. Sayão? Oh no they didn't know anything yet. They had just arrived. Dr. Sayão had fixed them up with a house. They had gotten married and had come to Brazil. They both had blue eyes and light curly hair, and fresh pink and white complexions. Their clothes looked crisp and clean. They walked out hand in hand looking into the jungle with shining eyes.

After we'd eaten the usual meal of rice and beans and meat we strolled around the village of Ceres. The highway cut through the bottom of a wide valley cleared halfway up the hillsides. In every direction among the treestumps straggled clumps of unfinished brick houses. Everywhere bricklayers were working, framing was going up. You caught glimpses against the sky of the bare brown backs of men setting the tiles on the roofs. That heap of bricks was going to be a moving picture theater; that one was going to be a bank. Here and there a little house already finished in white stucco with painted shutters stood out bright and neat. On all the hills around the great scraggly trees of the ruined jungle crowded rank on rank against the edges of the clearings.

We kept asking for Sayão. "He can't be far," people would smile and say.

Everybody was out that afternoon. The American Franciscans who had a little house beside the unfinished church were away on a mission. The young American who ran a brick kiln beside the highway in the middle of town had gone into Anápolis. The Americans who had set up the sawmill down by the river were off in São Paulo.

At Sayão's office, in the barracks next to the machine shop that kept his roadbuilding machinery in order, we tried to get a skinny young engineer to explain some of the workings of the colony to us but he begged off saying that Sayão would explain it so much better when he came.

Where the devil was Dr. Sayão?

One man pointed north, another pointed south. Out on the road at work. How could one tell?

A stocky little man, with long blond eartabs combed down from under a pith helmet, drove up in a jeep while we were talking. He spoke with authority. Sayão was in Amaro Leite. That meant sour milk. It was a town, a sort of a town. In the north, far in the north. He would be back this afternoon, he announced. *E certo.* How far was Amaro Leite? The stocky man spread out his arms. *Uma infinidade de leguas . . .* An infinity of leagues.

While we waited the judge and I went walking along the river. "This I suppose will be the principal *avenida,*" he was saying as we stumbled past wandering trucks through the deep dust. "They shouldn't cut down those trees. That should be the public garden right along the river."

All at once he was seized with a fury of cityplanning. He pointed here and there among the charred stumps, indicating parks and public buildings. I began to see columns sprouting among the trees, monuments to national heroes, bronze generals on horseback. The little judge's chest swelled.

We started across the floating bridge. The sun had set behind forested hills. In the hurried twilight of the tropics a slight coolness rose from the swift mustardgreen water.

"Soon there'll be a new bridge," said the judge proudly and pointed to the unfinished cement piers on the riverbank.

At the end of the bridge we met a very tall slender young man with fine sharpcut features and almost black skin. He wore the usual ragged workclothes. He grabbed the judge's hand and smiled with all his broken teeth. The judge asked him how he was doing, was he married yet, were there any pretty girls in the colônia? The young man talked fast and smiled some more and grabbed the lobe of his left ear with the thumb and forefinger of his right hand. That gesture meant O.K. He shook our hands again.

When we walked on the judge explained that this young fellow had been janitor at the courthouse in Goiânia. He'd been starving to death there on eight hundred cruzeiros a month. Now he was making fortyfive a day laying bricks. "The man is happy."

By the time we get back to the Grande Hotel Ceres it is so dark we have a hard time finding it. No word from Sayão. The dining room is jammed with men eating by the light of two lanterns and a candle. There are bearded men in hunting jackets who look like prospectors, there are salesmen and surveyors and engineers working on the road and the new bridge. Everybody is eating fast and talking fast. The dim light glints in eager eyes, on sweating cheekbones. When I grope my way out to the waterbucket to wash my face by the light of the lantern I see that the man ahead of me, a bullnecked character with a strawcolored beard, wears a large pearl earring in one ear. The night is already cool. From somewhere comes a smell of cape jessamine. Down in the dark valley an accordion is playing and a voice is singing a samba.

We are up at daylight standing around outside the office beside the repairshop in the valley with the construction foreman. There are bulldozers and road patrols. The place looks like a construction camp in the States. "No, he's not back yet."

"Yes he is," says the young man from São Paulo. "He got in from Amaro Leite at half past one . . . He'll be along any minute."

"Isn't it early?"

"He never gets tired. He sleeps while he drives."

The man with the helmet and the yellow eartabs drives up in his jeep. "He's back," he says in an excited tone. "His stomach is a little upset . . . He has a slight fever." The men crowd around the jeep with a look of concern on their faces. "But that is nothing . . . For Sayão that is nothing."

The Man Himself

A battered sedan drives up. There's a pretty girl on the front seat. The freshfaced man in khaki shirtsleeves behind the wheel seems hardly much older. As he steps to the ground we can see that he is a broadshouldered sixfooter. He shows even white teeth in a smile as he walks towards us. His step has a vigorous spring to it. He is older than he looked at a distance. There are thoughtful crowsfeet round his eyes. In fact the pretty girl is his daughter.

"Sayão, at your service," he says.

He rubs his hand over his rough chin and mutters apologetically that the barber is looking for him. He ate some beans and manioc flour in Amaro Leite that didn't set well. He isn't quite up to scratch this morning. He'll be all right. Let's go. He waves us into the back seat of the sedan and introduces the pretty girl as his eldest. Her father ought not to be out, she starts to tell us in remarkably good English, but she long ago gave up trying to do anything with him. He is incorrigible.

Sayão is talking to his men. He addresses a few words directly to each man in a pleasant offhand leisurely tone. Now and then he taps a man on the arm or lets a hand slide along his shoulders. When he turns towards us to step into the driver's seat we can see that he is a great deal older than he seemed at first glance. A man in his late forties. His eyes are a little bloodshot from the night driving yesterday. He swings the car around carelessly and drives down the highway. As he drives he leans back over the seat to tell us about the colônia.

Four years ago there was nothing. This was part of the federal government's colonization plan. Colonization was not his specialty. He's spent his life building roads. His pleasure has been in the fabrication of highways. It is the kind of outdoor life he likes.

"How many families have moved in already?" asks one of my companions.

"Around three thousand . . . This is cellular colonization, a lot of people crowding around a center . . ."

"The state land office says thirty thousand," interrupts the judge.

"That includes settlers outside the colônia . . . What we need, I'm beginning to think, is strip colonization, that is, to build roads and settle the land on either side . . ." Sayão swerves the car off the gravel and up a hill and stops on a grassy knoll in front of another unfinished building of raw brick. "This is our sugar mill. While we are waiting for the rest of the machinery we are going to use the generators to give light and power."

After looking through the mill we walk out among the hills of darkgreen corn sprouting vigorously out of the deep forest loam among the stumps and the charred trees so recently felled. "You see," Sayão explains, kicking at a stump a good four feet across, "we are not quite ready to use farm machinery. Our machines are hoes and the muscles in men's backs."

"How does a man ever get started hacking down the jungle?"

"I'll show you." As keen as a small boy with his first erector set, driving with one hand on the wheel through the rutted trails, he points out to us the various stages of colonization. He handles the battered sedan carelessly, the way a man might handle a well trained horse.

"The first year is hard," he explains. The newly arrived often camp out under a tree. Next they'll put up a bamboo shelter thatched with palm.

In the Brazilian backcountry there's a mutual aid system known as *mutirão*. You get together some food and *cachaça* and a guitar and invite the neighbors in. All the heaviest work is done that way. They'll work like fiends all day and in the evening they have a party.

Felling the tough hardwoods of the jungle is a man's work. Snakes are a peril. He tries to keep a stock of antitoxins sent up from São Paulo.

By the end of the year you are beginning to get enough food out of the crops of beans and rice and manioc you planted. Maybe you have something left over to sell, enough to buy shoes with. A couple of more years, if it's a hardworking family with plenty of children to help, you'll clear a little more land and sell the timber.

As he drives he points out little shacks in the clearings on either side of the valley. This man's from Minas. This one from Pernambuco. He brakes the car suddenly and calls to a man and a woman working in a field. João and Maria. They approach the car bashfully, a sunbaked couple with lean Arabian profiles. Sayão tells us they walked a thousand miles from some droughtstricken patch of ground in Ceará, God knows how many months it took them, on foot with their possessions on their heads, working their way as they came. "How are crops?" he asks them.

Their teeth flash as they smile in unison. "Here the land is cool, Mister Doctor," they chirrup. "We can grow rice without irrigation."

Sayão laughs happily. "They'll sell their rice at a profit," he says as he drives on. "When they get a little cash they'll buy bricks and build themselves a better house like that fellow over there."

He points out a little white house with an arched veranda, beside a clump of huge trees. "Then they'll clear more land and sell the timber to the sawmill and buy cattle . . . Coffee does magnificently here. We are planting Colombian type coffee for the American market. I want my settlers to plant coffee to tie them to the soil. A coffee plantation is a longterm investment . . . Brazilians are nomadic. They drift all over the continent. They'll clear a piece of land and plant a couple of crops on it and move on. I want my people to stay put . . ."

We drive on through raw plantations of coffee and corn and rice in jagged forest clearings. We visit the hospital and a small unfinished school.

The four things he needs to get a colony going, Sayão is saying as we walk about, are: first, an allweather road; second, proper division of the land so that each man knows what is his; third, a hospital and public health service; and, fourth, schools for the children. "But what I enjoy most is the road." He shows all his white teeth in a smile. "We are driving a road clear through the center of Brazil." He motions us back into the sedan.

Soon we have left the settlement behind and are charging north up the straight gravel road through the shaggy jungle. Sayão keeps turning back to talk to us as if he knew the road so well he didn't have to look at it. Sometimes he takes both hands off the wheel to make a gesture. The car plunges and swerves but he yanks it back without looking . . . "Here's where we get our gravel. The soil isn't so good. You can tell by the smaller size of the trees. Grazing land to be, but it's full of gravel . . . we get all we need for the road." Whenever he speaks of the road his voice takes on an affectionate tone as if he were speaking of one of his children.

"What do you do," the judge is asking, "when you get settlers who don't work?"

"When they don't want to work they leave. The others don't like to see idle people around. I've never had to use the police yet . . . or any kind of force. We argue with them, we give them friendly advice. But they have to work to eat. We are not running a home for incompetents. They soon catch the spirit of the thing. They see other people building houses, buying clothes, making money. Our people are natural colonizers."

We drive north for an hour at top speed. Blue mesas begin to rise up in the distance. Beyond the Rio São Patricio, Sayão turns into a construction camp. "Now, Papa, you can't go too far," the pretty daughter is insisting. "You have that government commission flying in this afternoon." He gives her the look of a small boy called in from a ballgame. "All right," he says, "but at least I can show them on the map."

The construction camp has an uptodate thrifty look. The living quarters are on trailers. The repairshop looks neat and businesslike. New lathes and Manley presses. Plenty of tools. The portable generators are humming. Everything is screened, there is electric light, a twoway radio.

In part of a shack fitted up as an office Sayão strides up to a map on the wall. He points with his forefinger to the mouths of the Amazon. "The object is to open up communications with Pará, our northern port will be the city of Belém. From São Paulo to Belém we have around twentyfour hundred kilometers to go. There are roads from São Paulo to Anápolis. On the new road from Anápolis we've come three hundred and forty."

He turns from the map to look us in the face with his hard level gaze. "Eventually we must have a road clear through to Belém. While we are waiting we'll carry the trucks by water on the Rio Tocantins. We are planning to use American landing barges, war surplus . . . we are negotiating for them in the States."

When he slams the car into the gravel again, Sayão hesitates at the turn as if he had half a mind to drive north anyway. "Now, Papa," says the pretty daughter. Obediently he points the car back the way we came. He twists his head around from the driver's seat and gives his guests a rueful smile. "You come back in a couple of years," he says, "and I'll drive you clear to Belém."

Bernardo Sayão had the greatest quality of leadership of any man I ever met. Building roads was his hobby and his obsession. According to his sisters even when he was small he showed a passion for outdoor life. He was born in Rio about the turn of the century of a welltodo family. He was raised in an atmosphere of achievement. His father went to work for the Central Railroad of Brazil when still a schoolboy and ended up as a director of the line. "A simple and straight career," Sayão said of his father one day with a proud smile. "He never lost his taste for the back country and neither did I."

Sayão's people lived on a sizable patch of hillside in the beautifully forested region of Tijuca that overlooks Rio and the bay and the great ocean beaches that stretch south from Copacabana. As soon as young Bernardo could walk he started roaming about the property with a sack of toys on his back looking for campsites. He'd play hooky from school to climb the conical basalt peaks that abound in the mountain ranges behind Rio. He was a firstrate soccerplayer and pulled a famous oar as an occasional member of the Botofogo Club rowing crews.

After graduating from the agricultural college at Piracicaba in the state of São Paulo he took a job under the Ministry of Agriculture. He married. His first wife died young, leaving him with two little girls to bring up. Already the Ministry of Agriculture was making plans, mostly on paper, for agricultural colonies to form centers of settlement for the back country people whose habit of life the officials in Rio considered distressingly nomadic. Sayão took them at their word. He worked to resettle the nomads, but his idea was that agricultural colonies would do no good without roads to bring their products to market.

Sayão became obsessed with the need for good roads to open up the hinterland. He went to work with such vim that he got in wrong with the agricultural bureaucrats who warmed chairs in Rio offices. His struggle with governmental red tape turned out to be as strenuous as his struggle to clear rights of way through the forest.

When Getúlio Vargas took over the national government in 1930 he too had ideas about colonizing the West. Friends told him of the candor and drive of the young athlete from Rio. The President sent word he wanted to see him.

Sayão's brotherinlaw, who arranged the details of the appointment, used to tell a story on him. Never much of a dresser, Bernardo had only one white suit. Since it was soiled he washed it himself, but he didn't have an iron to press it with. The suit was so rumpled that his brotherinlaw had to stop on the way to the presidential palace to buy Bernardo a new suit at a readymade clothing store. Vargas, already headed for the dictatorship, knew a good man when he saw one. He started Sayão on the work of setting up experimental farms. He encouraged his interest in western Goiás.

About the time of the Second World War, when Sayão married again, the first question he asked his betrothed was, would she mind living out in the bush? It was Vargas who arranged his appointment to manage a projected agricultural colony in the red soil region among the tributaries of the Rio Tocantins.

His daughters still tell of the caravan of fortyeight trucks and jeeps which Sayão led on the great trek across country to the Rio das Almas. When the expedition reached the river, there was of course no bridge. The lands assigned for settlement lay on the other side. Sayão threw off his clothes and swam across. The current was so swift that an associate who tried to follow him was drowned.

Sayão's first job was to bridge the river. He used gasoline drums lashed together and covered by a rough board roadway. For years he carried on a vendetta with the government bureau that was trying to get these gasoline drums back to the oil companies that claimed ownership. Sayão said he could not give up his drums until he had finished a proper concrete bridge across the river. At the same time he pushed through a road to the railhead at Anápolis. This road opened up an immense region of fertile country. By the time it was finished and hardsurfaced Anápolis had doubled in size and Ceres was a city of forty thousand people.

Sayão fought the Rio bureaucracy at every step. The ministry kept demanding explanations and sending out investigating committees to plague him. They couldn't understand a man who worked for the sport of it with no thought of accumulating a fortune for himself and his family. His instructions were to build a set of agricultural buildings and barns for a model cattle farm. Instead he'd built a road and bridged a river. He wanted houses for his settlers, not offices for officials. The idea of sitting in an office made him sick. He lived in his car the way the oldtime pioneers lived on horseback.

Not too long after my visit to Sayão back in 1948 he became so irked by bureaucratic obstructions and frustrations that he threw up his job with the government. He went to work on a farm in the State of Rio de Janeiro. The farm had a stone quarry. He got out the rock himself and trucked it in person to his customers. In his spare time, just for his own satisfaction, he paved the local roads.

His name was legendary in western Goiás. In 1953 a delegation sought him out, at a location near Belo Horizonte where he was building a road, to beg him to run for lieutenant governor. When it was explained to him that the lieutenant governor was in charge of the state road program he consented to run. He was elected by an enthusiastic majority.

He immediately went to work on the highway that linked the state capital at Goiânia with the milling and cheesemaking center at Anápolis. He improved communications through to São Paulo. All the while he dreamed of the road to Belém.

When Juscelino Kubitschek's administration inaugurated the project to build a national capital a hundred miles to the northeast of Goiânia, in the enormous tract of tableland that had been long since set aside for a federal district to replace the region around Rio, he remembered the great roadbuilder. Sayão was appointed one of the working directors of Novacap, the government corporation entrusted with the work of construction. He would not take the post until his old friend, Israél Pinheiro, who as president of Novacap was in charge of the operation, promised that he would never be expected to set foot in an office.

As director of Novacap, Sayão for the first time had sufficient funds and proper assistants. Hardsurface roads had to be completed to Belo Horizonte to the east and to Anápolis and Goiânia to the south; but the project into which he put his heart and soul was the nine hundred and fifty mile road, stretching due north through barely explored territory, that was to open up passage from central Brazil to the seaports and mining regions in the mouths of the Amazon.

When I was being shown around the construction work in Brasília in the summer of 1958 I tried in every way to catch up with Sayão. He was off in the bush, we were told. One of his chauffeurs drove us around, in a car, he explained with awe in his voice, that Dr. Sayão often rode in. He pointed out the plain frame house where Sayão lived, a place where he had once eaten a meal, a chair he had sat in. When he learned that I had spent several days in Dr. Sayão's company several years before he treated my wife and me with almost embarrassing respect. Some of the mana of the great roadbuilder had rubbed off on us.

In January 1959, a few days before the bulldozers working up from the south were to meet the bulldozers coming down from Belém to open the final link in the preliminary trail of the Belém road, Sayão was killed by a falling tree. He was directing the clearing of the dense rainforest near Imperatriz on the Rio Tocatins in the State of Maranhão. He had sat down for a moment at a rough table to check something on his map when the tree fell on him and crushed his skull. He died very soon.

The *candongos,* as they call the roadworkers and construction workers, revered him as a father. He was a saint who worked miracles. His death was the end of the world. One of his jeep drivers, Benedito Segundo, fell dead when he heard the news.

Bernardo Sayão and Benedito Segundo were the first men buried in the new cemetery at Brasília. The whole city was in mourning. People walked along the streets crying. Particularly the huts of the candongos were hung with crepe. The candongos begged that Dr. Sayão be buried standing up, with his face to the north, so that he could look forever up the great highway he had planned.

III

A NATION IN SEARCH OF A CAPITAL

The Madmen of the Planalto

"Mad," growled Israél Pinheiro affectionately, when I first asked him about his friend the roadbuilder. We were at the Santos Dumont Airport in Rio in the pearly dawn of an August Sunday in 1958, waiting to take off for Brasília. "Of course he's a little mad."

Dr. Israél, as everybody calls him, is a rangy grayhaired quizzical man with a long rough-hewn countenance and a determined jaw under a clipped gray mustache. His tart manner tends to be mellowed by the play of expression on his face and by his sudden way of showing his long teeth in a dour smile to emphasize a joke. ". . . And so am I," he added, "and so's Kubitschek." He grinned. "That's why we get along so well. It takes madmen to put through a project like Brasília."

We climb aboard and the Beechcraft roars into the air and circles over the city's closepacked apartment buildings, which overtop dense parks and gardens tufted with royal palms and the bay, duncolored this morning and full of shipping; all enclosed in Rio's fantastic frame of conical mountains and foaming white beaches. Above the abrupt crenelated mountain range which seems to be forever pressing the teeming city back into the ocean, the pilot sets his course into the north-west.

After the throngs and the jangling traffic and the brawling voices of loudspeakers and the dense humidity of the seaport it's a delight to breathe the cool sharp air at six thousand feet. The checkerboard below is the resort city of Petrópolis, where the betteroff people of Rio spend their weekends among upland breezes. Beyond appears the deep gorge of the Paraíba, a river laced with rapids. There are textile factories set in criss-cross patches of industrial towns on the plains beyond the mountains. Volta Redonda, where the steel mills are, is lost under the clouds to the left. To the right I catch a glimpse of Juíz de Fora, a textile town I spent a night in years ago. More mills, railroad yards . . . The plane bores into a high overcast.

At the end of an hour the Beechcraft is out in the sunshine again, flying over an enormous empty landscape. Small muddy watercourses wind between eroded hills. No, the green patches are not pasture, Dr. Israél explains, it's a wild grass with little nutriment. He's a stockman as well as a builder of cities. "Further west the grass is better." The brightgreen oblongs now are sugarcane. "See: not a house, plenty of room for develop-ment," he shouts with a creaky laugh.

"President Kubitschek says there's half an inhabitant to the square kilometer. I can't even see half an inhabitant." "Wait till we finish Brasília," Dr. Israél leans back in his seat to talk into my ear. "Every half will turn into ten."

He pours a stack of glossy promotional literature into my lap: Brazil's new capital in four languages.

Since the beginning of its existence as a separate nation, Brazil has been in search of a capital. The forerunners of in-dependence in the late seventeen hundreds dreamed already of a federal city in the interior. At the convention which con-firmed the setting up of a constitutional monarchy in 1823 Brasília was suggested as a name for the future capital. In

1891 the convention which established the charter for a federal republic on the model of the United States of the North set aside an area of four hundred and forty square leagues on the high plateau far west of the sweltering coastal lowlands as the eventual governing center of the Brazilian union. The constitution of 1946 laid down the manner in which the transfer of the capital should be carried out. When Juscelino Kubitschek was elected President ten years later he determined to make that long projected capital a reality.

Kubitschek was the son of a middle-European immigrant and a Brazilian mother. Like Dr. Israél he came from Minas Gerais. He was born in the secluded little city of Diamantina, which generations before had been the center of a great diamond industry. During Kubitschek's boyhood years the place was a remote and forgotten settlement shrunken into a straggle of rambling old colonial buildings amid the scorched hills. Young Juscelino had no money behind him. A hardworking eager young man, he managed to get himself into the medical school in Belo Horizonte, the new capital of his state.

Belo Horizonte (Beautiful Horizon)—the Brazilians are fond of rhetorical names—was the first important Brazilian city to be built right off the drafting board. The people of Minas Gerais, Mineiros they call themselves, decided in the early nineteen hundreds that they needed a new state capital. Their old capital, Ouro Prêto (Black Gold) was, like Diamantina, an ancient colonial burgh where old families vegetated amid the superannuated splendors of convents and palaces and churches built in the days when the exploitation of great deposits of gold and precious stones brought wealth into these torrid uplands. All that was in the past. Now the raising of zebu cattle and corn and sugar cane and upland rice; manufacturing and the iron mountain at Itabira offered prospects of a new prosperity. Instead of gold and diamonds the Mineiros were beginning to dream of virgin lands to the westward.

The "beautiful horizon" the new state capital looked out on was the Brazilian west: the fertile river valleys running north into the Amazon and south into the Paraná and Paraguay rivers and the high plateau of Goiás and the wilderness of Mato Grosso.

The founding of Belo Horizonte was greeted by howls of derision from the rest of the country. Can't be done, the wiseacres said; you can't take a city off a drafting board and bring it to life. The wiseacres were wrong; the venture was successful. It was during Kubitschek's student days that the city really began to take hold. Industries sprang up, the population grew. Already in 1958 Belo Horizonte had more than half a million inhabitants, bristled with skyscrapers and shining white apartmentbuildings, and was considered the pleasantest city in Brazil to live in.

So the idea that a city could be invented on the drafting board was nothing new to Dr. Kubitschek. After some studies in Paris and a successful career as one of Belo Horizonte's leading urologists he was appointed mayor by Getúlio Vargas. From mayor of the state capital it was an easy step to governor of the state.

The Mineiros man one of Brazil's smoothest political machines. They are a stubborn and clannish people with a sharp eye for the main chance; a man has to fight hard for a living among those scraggly hills. In the period of confusion and recrimination that followed Getúlio Vargas's melodramatic suicide the Socialist Democratic party of Minas brought forth Dr. Kubitschek as their candidate for the presidency of Brazil. He was a new man, a progressive technician with his face towards the west, a doctor of medicine who was free from political entanglements. He was elected by an honest majority: Brasília was one of the planks in his platform.

"We have seen the success of our own new capital," said Kubitschek and his friends. "Here's our chance to build a federal capital that will unite the whole nation."

People had made a lot of money out of the rise in real estate values in Belo Horizonte. The knowledge that their whole state lay athwart the lines of communication between Brasília and the sea heightened the enthusiasm of the leading Mineiros for the project. Kubitschek became their man with a mission. He would go down in history as the President who finally achieved the century old ambition for a new capital.

Two years before Kubitschek's inauguration as President the Brazilian Congress had appointed a commission to choose the best site in the federal rectangle. This commission contracted with the firm of Donald J. Belcher & Associates of Ithaca, N.Y., for a survey. A group of American engineers and geologists, most of them from Cornell, recommended five possible locations that offered the climate, the water supply, the drainage, the subsoil necessary for the foundation of a large city. The Brazilian commission chose the present site of Brasília as the best.

When the problem of city planning and architecture arose President Kubitschek could think only of Niemeyer. His name has been associated with Kubitschek's for years. It was Oscar Niemeyer's design for the resort suburb of Pampulha, which Kubitschek promoted while he was mayor of Belo Horizonte, that made him the best known of the young Brazilian architects.

The novel style of these buildings raised a storm. Kubitschek stood by his architect and stubbornly invited him to design a municipal theater. Even the fact that Niemeyer calls himself a Communist while Kubitschek usually defends private enterprise did not interfere with their collaboration. When the President offered Niemeyer the post of Supervisor of Construction at Brasília at a salary which amounted to only a few hundred dollars a month, Niemeyer is said to have turned down wellpaying contracts with private interests to take the job. "Niemeyer," Brazilians will tell you, "is the soul of Kubitschek."

Brazilian politicians are notoriously easy of access. In those days it wasn't too hard for an American to get an interview with President Kubitschek, particularly if the American were a journalist and the subject was Brasília.

I was taken to see him at eight o'clock in the morning at the Larangeiras Palace in Rio. It was raining hard out of a sagging gray sky; chilly; Rio was having one of its rare touches of winter. This palace which Kubitschek chose for his official residence was built early in the century by a family that owned docks in Santos during the great coffee boom. Parisian architects and decorators decked it out with all the pomp they could dream up as a background for the patriarchal Brazilian capitalism of that day. There were marble columns and salmoncolored hangings. Gilt cupids crawled around the edges of the mirrors. There were massive overmantles, plush sofas, and oriental rugs. A gilded grand piano stood out on the parquet floor under an enormous chandelier. The gray light streaky with rain poured through the tall windows, glittered in the crystals, and made the huge drawingroom seem unbelievably empty.

When President Kubitschek came walking with a short springy stride, keeping step with his chief of protocol, he looked almost as out of place as his visitors amid these Frenchified splendors. There was a certain small town look about the way he wore his clothes which was not unattractive to an American. He held himself well. He was taller than I had expected, a sallow man with large prominent eyes. Even before we sat down on the sofa he came right to the point.

"You are going to Brasília?" He pronounced the name with a special sort of fervor. He started right away to explain that Brasília was not a luxury; it was a necessity. If Brazil were to go on progressing at the rate it had been progressing during the past ten years the center of population must move westward and northward; the nation needed a crossroads.

The President talked clearly and ardently. Occasionally he stopped to allow the friend who had accompanied me to translate a difficult phrase into English. As he talked he sketched out a map of Brazil so clearly I could almost see it on the wall behind the gilded piano. Sixtyfive million people. Twenty states and four territories. Roughly half the land area of South America and most of it empty. He described how the riversystems of the Amazon basin bound Brazil on the north, more fresh water pouring out through equatorial rainforests than in all the other rivers of the world put together, thousands of kilometers navigable by ocean steamers. Still the only practical communication between Belém, the old Portuguese city which was the port of entry of the Amazon region, and the rest of the country was by air.

"The construction of Brasília is already forcing us to build roads," he said. Communication with São Paulo and the south was already open. The highway from Rio was just about finished. The Belém-Brasília road now under construction was being built through regions that weren't even mapped. Already they were cutting through forests of trees forty meters high. His gesture gave an inkling of the slow fall óf an enormous tree. I explained I had met Sayão ten years before. He nodded enthusiastically.

Subsidiary roads, he went on, would link that highway with the Atlantic coast. With his hand he indicated the eastward bulge towards Africa. With his forefinger he drew a line along the string of isolated coastal cities running southeast from Natal and Fortaleza to Bahia and Rio and São Paulo and down into the temperate regions of Rio Grande do Sul that border on Uruguay and the Argentine.

Along the coast, he explained, the country averaged twenty-five inhabitants to the square kilometer. Brazil, socially and economically, was still only a long narrow seaside strip like Chile. "Inland we only have half an inhabitant," he said with a wry smile.

He turned to look me full in the face. "During your pioneer days," he said, "you North Americans always had the Pacific Ocean for a goal to lure you on across the mountains. That's why you populated your part of the continent so quickly. Our way west has been barred by impenetrable forests and by the Andes. Brasília will constitute a goal, a place to head for on the high plateau. Building Brasília means roads. A movement of population into the fine farmlands of the interior is already going on. As soon as I was inaugurated President, I gave the word to start construction. The Brazilian people demand a new capital. Brasília is the great goal of my administration."

The President was dropping into a political oration. I could half imagine the crowded hall, the wardheelers leading the applause of the crowd, the flash of the cameras, the busy pencils of the notetaking journalists.

He caught himself suddenly and asked for comprehension by a broad deprecatory sweep of his hands. There was a pause. The director of protocol cleared his throat. It was time to leave. We rose for the formalities of leavetaking.

Dr. Israél filled in the rest of the story. Construction started in the spring of 1956, when the President appointed him head of Novacap, the government corporation more or less modeled on TVA which was set up by Congress to put through the work.

Dr. Israél, so his secretary told me on the side, was chosen because he had made a conspicuous success of the management of the Rio Doce Railroad after its purchase from the British during the war. Dr. Israél came of a prominent and popular family in the northwest of Minas. His father had served as state governor. A graduate of the School of Mines at Ouro Prêto, Dr. Israél was associated with Kubitschek's projects in Belo Horizonte. As a public speaker he was famous for his amusing stories. Now in the summer of 1958 he was spending alternate weeks in his Rio office and at construction headquarters on the *planalto*.

So, this cloudy August morning, it is the Novacap Beechcraft which is speeding my wife and me and Dr. Israél and his wife, Dona Cora, on an excursion to visit the construction work on the new capital.

Political Fences

Already we are beyond Belo Horizonte. Some time ago the copilot pointed out a light smudge of smoke blurring the city's clustered buildings on the northern horizon. Now Dr. Israél turns towards me and jabs at the window between us with a long forefinger. "The road, the road," he shouts above the rumble of the twin motors. Sure enough a red gash cuts across the landscape from horizon to horizon. What look like tiny white caterpillars are finished concrete bridges. "The highroad from Belo Horizonte to Brasília," he shouts exultantly. "Brasília's lifeline."

The plane drones on across higher drier hills where trails are faint and few. The rivers are clear green now, the sky clear blue above ranks of cottony clouds. The earth is very red, vaguely stained with verdigris where water flows.

The plane starts to bank. On the spinning tippedup landscape a few vague squares appear, streets, tileroofed houses, fenced fields. Buzzards cruise above. This is the town of João Pinheiro, named after Dr. Israél's father. The pilot circles over what looks like a plowed field. When he lands the strip turns out just as bumpy as it looked from the air.

Groups of swarthy countrymen come forward to greet Dr. Israél, backcountry politicos, candongos, young engineers in white shirts and khaki pants. They have a scorched look from the dry upland sun. Their faces wear easy smiles. Their voices are lowpitched and cordial. They shake hands a little shyly. We all file out through a stile in a thorny redflowering hedge that keeps the cattle off the airstrip.

Dr. Israél takes charge. He packs us into jeeps and pickup trucks that string out into a procession along the new highway. Not surfaced yet. You can hardly see it for the driving red dust as we drive over mile after mile. The road lacks bridges; but already a determined motorist, so I'm told, can make his way in good weather from Belo Horizonte to Brasília. "A road means life," Dr. Israél cries out.

We are ushered into a neat building at the edge of a dry gulch which the highway engineers have built themselves for a messhall. Tiny glasses of cachaça are brought out on trays. Congratulations are in order. *Felicidades.* Toasts. Dr. Israél makes a short speech.

Down in the gully below the messhall, plank tables have been laid out under a piece of aluminum roofing set on tall poles to let the breeze blow through. It's a *churrasco*, a barbeque; in Maryland we'd call it a bull roast. There's a smell of frizzling meat. Along a shallow trench full of smoldering hardwood, chunks of beef broil on long iron spikes. At the end a suckling pig on a spit revolves slowly above the coals.

Around the fringes, forming a smiling corridor as the guests are ushered through, bronze, mustard, tobaccocolored, tan to ruddy, are the packed faces of the candongos who are gravely waiting their turn. They have on their best straw hats, their best clean Sunday shirts. Brown eyes squint in the dazzle of sun as they peer into the shadow under the aluminum roof to watch the proceedings.

Dr. Israél bustles about with an expert air making exploratory cuts with his pocketknife into the broiling beef. Ay, he complains, some of it is tough.

He shrugs and includes in one halfapologetic gesture all the countryside crowding in about the tables. "Politics," he whispers in my ear. "How do you say in America?" he asks with his creaky laugh. "Poleetical fences?"

He straightens himself up, suddenly quite serious. The

greatness of all this is the road, he is telling the candongos.
Politicians come and go but the road will continue.

He leans over to cut a couple of strips of crackling off the
roasting pig and hands them with a disarming grin to his
guests. "Tell them back in America what a road means in
Brazil."

An attentive little man brings us heaped plates. The upland
air makes for an appetite. As soon as the throngs begin to
back off from the ravaged tables Dr. Israél has us on our way
back to the airstrip. He is explaining that he wants us to see
Paracatu, the town his wife, Dona Cora's family came from.

The airstrip in Paracatu is too short even for the Beechcraft,
so a small singlemotor job has flown in to take us there. My
wife and I get to whispering and tittering together as we
squeeze into seats in the tiny plane. What strikes us funny
is how similar the political goings on at the churrasco were to
what would be happening at a political oyster roast back in
the northern neck of Virginia where we come from. The language, the costumes, the skintints are different, but the basic
behavior, the jockeyings for position, the prestige of family,
the playing up to local prejudices are so much the same that
it's laughable. This is the sort of country politicking we have
at home. Under all the differences there are similarities between the Brazilian and the North American forms of democracy. I try to explain to Dr. Israél that we ought to get along
because we have so many of the same vices but neither his
English nor my Portuguese can carry the weight of my explanation. The pilot has his motor roaring so we can't hear
anything anyway. We grin and make funny faces at each
other and we're airborne again.

The plane follows the red streak of the road, blurred with
dust where bulldozers are at work. Again the emptiness of
eroded brown hills. Soon the little plane is circling over a
green field. There's a river. Dr. Israél points out washouts in
the red clay where people years ago panned gold out of the

creek beds. Canebrakes, bananatrees, a few mangoes and papayas among narrow tiled roofs faded gray with age. Hardly a sign of crops. "What on earth do they live on," we feel like asking, "in Paracatu?"

An ancient rattletrap Chevrolet is waiting. Dr. Israél bundles us into it. The cobbled alleys of this little town weren't built for cars. They are steep and narrow. Sunscorched ponies are tethered outside of every store. Brown countrymen ride past under broad hats. A team of four yokes of white oxen comes lounging magnificently through the dust. The place has a look of tightened belts, poverty, and nakedness. It swarms with flies. Dr. Israél is explaining that this is what all the back country is like before the highway comes.

Years and years ago they had gold. Then they had hunger. Soon they will have the highway.

With a shudder and a gasp the Chevrolet rattles to a stop in the central square opposite the church. The Franciscans operate a school there. We have a short talk with the schoolmaster, an earnest young Hollander who speaks a little English. Meanwhile Dona Cora has gone off in search of antiques: already we share her admiration for the simple elegance and the solid construction of the colonial furniture still to be picked up in these parts "for a song."

We go along while Dr. Israél pays a call on a dreamylooking blond man who is evidently the local precinct boss for the Social Democrats. We sit in his parlor drinking cafezinhos and listening politely while he and Dr. Israél talk hurried politics in sibilant halfwhispers.

Disheveled little boys stare at us with grave gray eyes through the tall barred window that lets in the light off the square. A flock of them. They all are sandyhaired like their father. Our host looks too young to have produced so many. My Lord how many children people have in this country! "How do you ever feed them?" we feel like asking.

The two Brazilians remember their guests and make the

conversation general. The road, they expain, will pass close to Paracatu. It will mean prosperity, rising land values, every house in town will be worth more. There will be buses, trucks to ship crops out, stores to buy things in, probably a bank. The eyes of the precinct boss mist with emotion as he points towards his boys who are pushing their pale faces against the bars in the window. "These," he says, "will have a better life than I have had."

Handicaps to Development

On the way back to the airstrip Dr. Israél begins to talk about that bank. A branch bank would be established, but what good would it do? The great roadblock to development throughout the country was the high cost of money. Suppose that fellow we'd been talking to wanted to set up some small factory that would employ people and give them much needed wages, he'd have to have funds. A bank would charge him twenty or thirty per cent interest, partly to cover inflation, but partly out of the old habits of medieval usury. Nobody could start a small enterprise under such a handicap. What impressed Dr. Israél most last time he'd visited the States was the cheap interest rates. No wonder we were so prosperous in North America.

Now he himself is a man—he gives us one of his famous grins—tolerably wellknown in the community. He ought to be what we called in America "a good credit risk," but, not too long ago, he tried to borrow money to buy some cattle. He owns family lands out in this corner of the state that will only produce grazing every few years when the rainfall is sufficient. Well, an unusual rainfall gave abundant grass but when he'd tried to borrow money to buy cattle to eat it . . . impossible. There wasn't much margin of profit in fattening cattle anyway. He found he couldn't borrow the money to buy them at any interest rate that would make a profit possible . . . If he was in such a dilemma think of the poor man . . . and as close as Belo Horizonte there was a shortage of beef!

On the way back to the airstrip we pick up Dona Cora. "Good hunting?" Dr. Israél asks in mock despair. She nods. "Ay, ay." Dr. Israél claps his hand to his wallet. "A pain in the pocketbook."

Construction Site

After Paracatu the pilot follows the red streak of the new road. Where bulldozers are at work the sharp line blurs with dust. Again the emptiness of eroded hills. No trails now. We are flying over a wilderness of low shrubs and sourlooking flat lands spotted with round ponds left over from the last rains. After crossing into the state of Goiás the motors roar. The plane has begun to climb. The scrambled hills of Minas Gerais straighten out into the long hogbacks of the high plateau. The air is cooler.

Suddenly the road appears again. It's a paved road now with traffic on it. Crossroads. Roads in every stage of completion. Cars, trucks, jeeps, buses move back and forth. The plane skirts a long ridge that bristles with scaffolding, concrete construction, cranes, bulldozers, earthmoving machinery. A file of dumptrucks parades down the center.

Dr. Israél points through the window. "Brasília." He smiles and shrugs and frowns all at once. The shanty town unfolding below is known as Cidade Livre, the free city, a straggle of frame buildings painted in a dozen colors on either side of a broad dusty road. He insists on calling it "the provisional city." In two or three years it will have done its work. They'll tear it down. "The real city will take its place."

Dr. Israél makes his pilot bank steeply to show his guests the beginnings of a dam in a shallow gorge where two broad valleys come together. That, he announces, is where the main power plant will be. He points in two directions with his arms, a swimming gesture: "All this is lake."

At the point where the foundations of the city jut out into the future lake the broad windows of Niemeyer's presidential palace glitter in the afternoon sun. They call it the Palace of the Dawn. Its strange columns gleam like a row of white kites set upside down. Off to the right the windows of the long low tourist hotel balance airily above the shadow of its open lower story. To the left rise the boxlike shapes of apartments and crisscross blocks of small concrete residences. The little white tentlike building on the brow of the hill is a church.

Already the plane is taxiing across the surfaced runways of the airport.

"The main landing strip will be 3300 meters long," says Dr. Israél proudly as he ushers us into the temporary passenger terminal. "Already five airlines have established commercial flights to all parts of Brazil."

The terminal is full of men in work clothes, candongos, engineers, machine operators, a few wives and children. Clothing, faces, baggage are stained with red dust.

"Brasília will have the first airport in the world specially designed for the age of jets," Dr. Israél continues. "It is the first city planned from the air."

As Dr. Israél piloted us through the future city we had trouble distinguishing what was really there from what was going to be there. It was like visiting Pompeii or Monte Alban, but in reverse. Instead of imagining the life that was there two thousand years ago we found ourselves imagining the life that would be there ten years hence.

The Brasília Palace Hotel was almost complete. Comfortable beds, airy rooms. Hot and cold water, electric light. To be sure the silence of the plateau was broken at night by the sound of hammering and sawing on the annex they are building out back and by the swish of shovels of men at work spreading soil for a garden between the restaurant's glass wall and the curving edges of the tiled swimming pool.

Niemeyer's strange mania for underground entrances has saddled the hotel with an unnecessarily inconvenient lobby. It surprised us to find in a pupil of Le Corbusier's functionalism so little regard for the necessary functions of a building. In case of fire, we asked each other, how would we ever get out?

The presidential palace we found to be a singularly beautiful building of glass and white concrete, built long and low to fit into the long lines of the hills on the horizon, floating as lightly as a flock of swans on broad mirroring pools of clear water that flanked the entrance. The inner partitions were glass too. We did ask each other where, amid all those glass walls, the poor President could find a spot to change his trousers or a private nook to write a letter in.

From the palace we drove on a wide highway to what was to correspond to Capitol Hill in Washington: The Triangle of the Three Powers they called it. An enormous open space. Draglines were leveling the red clay hills. Drills like gigantic corkscrews were boring for the foundation piling. Here would rise the circular halls for the Senate and House and a pair of tileshaped steel and glass buildings behind to house their offices. These would be balanced by a building for the Supreme Court and another for the executive departments. From there a broad mall with many roadways would run between rows of ministries to the downtown center where the banks and the hotels and the theaters and the department stores were to be established. From this center, "like the wings of a jet plane," in Lucio Costa's words, were to stretch in either direction blocks of apartment buildings and private residences. To form the tail of the plane a continuation of the mall would stretch for miles in the direction of the eventual railroad station and the industrial suburbs.

There was not to be a traffic light in the city. Every intersection was to be by overpass or underpass. Unobstructed
roadways would feed the traffic into the center of each block
where ample parking space was foreseen under the open un-
derstories of the buildings. Automobile traffic would come
in from the rear. The front of every apartment building or
private house was to open on a landscaped square. Shopping
centers on the North American suburban plan were to be
built within walking distance of each residential block so that
the paths for pedestrians would be separate from the automobile roads.

We found ourselves imagining the buildings to be, the
great paved spaces, the lawns and gardens, the serried louvers
and trellises shading the windows from the sun, the gleaming
walls of tile and glass.

"This is the underground bus terminal," said Dr. Israél,
patting a wall of smooth red clay affectionately with his hand.
"Escalators will take people up to the great paved central platform above . . . To the left is the theater and restaurant district . . . a little Montmartre."

He bursts into his creaky laugh.

"Of course you think we're mad. A man has to be a little
mad to get anything accomplished in Brazil."

His quarrel with his American engineers, he began to explain, was that they were not mad enough. They were help-
ful and practical but they were so accustomed to perfect machinery they had forgotten how to improvise. "In the old
days you Americans were the greatest improvisers in the
world." In Brazil everything had to be improvised.

He went on to tell one of his favorite stories. Once when
he was running the Rio Doce Company a flood took the piers
out from under a steel bridge. Traffic stopped. If the ore
stopped going out, the dollars stopped coming in. His American engineers said they could repair the bridge all right but
they'd have to wait for a crane to come from the States. That

crane would have taken months even if he'd had the dollars to buy it. Among the work gangs he found a gigantic Negro who said he knew how to get the bridge back on its piers without a crane . . .

I'd seen the great oxen in the Rio Doce? I nodded. Yes, I'd seen eleven yokes hitched together. How could one forget the great teams of oxen straining forward with the pondered magnificence of a frieze on an early Greek temple? . . .

Well, he went on excitedly, with a hundred oxen and levers and jacks and winches that illiterate Negro had the bridge open for traffic in nineteen days . . . "Improvise . . . that is my answer when people tell me that trying to build a capital out here on the plateau is a crazy project . . . Central Brazil must have roads, it must have buildings . . . out of sheer necessity we are improvising Brasília."

The Boomtown Feeling

We found that the contagion of Dr. Pinheiro's enthusiasm had infected the contractors and their engineers and foremen. The place steamed with boomtown excitement. "We all feel ten years younger than when we came," was how his middle-aged secretary, Dr. Quadros, put it.

Dr. Quadros' niece, Leonora Quadros, invited us to dinner at her small house out beyond the great compounds of the construction companies that covered the hillside across from the Novacap administration building. She was a handsome young woman of twentyeight. To our amazement we found that she was managing her father's building materials business.

"That's not the American idea of a Brazilian girl, now, is it?" she asked with a teasing smile. "In a new city everybody gets a chance."

"It's the need to improvise new ways of doing things that keeps us on our toes," says the young man who was introduced as Brasília's oldest inhabitant; he arrived even before they built Dom Bosco's shrine.

Dom Bosco was an Italian missionary friar who prophesied a great civilization for the central uplands of Brazil. They had taken him for Brasília's patron saint.

Asked if he intends to stay, the oldest inhabitant nods vigorously: "My life has become Brasília," he says.

The young people around Leonora Quadros' table seemed to have enlisted in the building of the city as you might enlist in a military campaign: for the duration. According to them the miracle was that construction had started at all. The city had advanced too far to be abandoned now, they insisted.

An American concern, Raymond Concrete and Pile, was already at work on the dam and the powerplant and the buildings for the eleven ministries. Business interests in São Paulo were vitally engaged. At least five important firms from Rio were involved. In all more than fifty Brazilian concerns were under contract for various phases of the work. A location had been chosen for an American embassy. The steel girders for the congress buildings were already arriving from the States.

Round the table they all talked at once. They showered us with statistics. Already forty thousand people at work. The hotel only took twelve months to complete; the palace, thirteen. In twenty months twelve million cubic feet of earth had been excavated. Two hundred and sixty kilometers of paved roads had been built, and more than six hundred kilometers of dirt roads.

Roads meant settlers. Already the administration of Novacap was at its wit's end to find ways of keeping settlers out before housing could be found for them.

"How can you build an entire city in two years?"

The Oldest Inhabitant answered patly that two years ago nobody would have dreamed that Brazilians would win the world's soccer championship. To complete Brasília would mean the world's championship in city planning and modern architecture.

Everybody laughed when he proclaimed that architecture would outrank football as a national sport. Her architecture is the soul of the new Brazil, he insisted. That's why he considered President Kubitschek a great man; because he understood the three basic impulses behind Brazilian progress: new roads, new cities, new buildings.

When Kubitschek's choice of an architect came up everybody started arguing hammer and tongs about Niemeyer. Niemeyer's buildings were impractical, said one. His work was magnificent, said another. The rafters rang with argument. "Niemeyer is only interested in how his buildings look from the outside," said Dona Leonora in a ringing voice. "He keeps dumping insoluble problems in the lap of his engineers and contractors . . . He's not an architect at all. He's a sculptor, a sculptor with building materials."

This statement brought an approving silence round the table.

A *Sculptor with Building Materials*

Niemeyer has remained a center of argument in Brazil.

When I met him at his workshop in Rio the first thing that struck me was his bashfulness. A small sober dishfaced man with mistrustful eyes. His married daughter had already presented him with a grandchild. Like so many Brazilians he looked younger than he was, but he must have been about fifty.

If you asked him a question he would throw away the answer the way an Englishman would. In a nation of voluble people he seemed remarkably chary of words. It was only after talking to him for some time that I began to notice a sort of broadshouldered assurance about him, like a bricklayer's or stonemason's assurance. There was a craftsman's

sharp definition about the way he used his hands. When he
did speak it seemed straight from the heart. He was completely without side.

All sorts of European strains make up his family tree.
Friends tell you that he had a random kind of youth.
Couldn't keep his mind on his schooling. He dabbled in
sports. He did have a taste for drawing, but it wasn't until
he married at twentytwo that he took up architecture, and
that, some cynics claim, was because his fatherinlaw was a
contractor.

More likely his dedication to architecture stems from his
association with Lucio Costa, who for a while was director of
the School of Fine Arts in Rio. Lucio Costa has Socrates'
gift for infecting young people with his enthusiasms. At the
time when Niemeyer studied with him modern architecture
had already become the passion of his life. Niemeyer went
to work in Lucio Costa's drafting room. From then on there
was no further doubt as to where Niemeyer's career lay.

He used to claim he took architecture up as a sport, the
way a man might take up soccer. Since his taking on the job
of architect for Brasília he has sobered considerably. He even
recently admitted in one of his rare public statements that
this heavy responsibility had made him understand that the
time had come to give up some of the freakish and playful
experiments—Bohemianism, he called them—of his early
work. Now he must pay more attention to construction.

Like most people who do first rate work in the arts
Niemeyer thinks, feels and lives entirely in the terms of his
craft. He likes to live well but he doesn't care for money.
About politics he is disconcertingly naïve. Though he claims
to be a Communist and contributes to the Party war chest he
designs churches and yachtclubs and gambling casinos with
as much enthusiasm as he does workers' apartments. His
last work in Rio before leaving for Brasília was to finish the

maquette for the crownshaped structure in glass and stressed concrete he planned for a national cathedral.

His domestic life is that of a middleclass Brazilian. He's sluggish about many practical things. Like Parisians and Manhattanites, the Cariocas—as the people of Rio call themselves—can't imagine living anywhere else than in their beautifully situated, overcrowded city. Niemeyer has the typical Carioca's dread of travel. During his last days in Rio he seemed to be thinking more about how much he hated to leave his family and the pleasant dwelling he designed for himself, in the mountain valley high above one of Rio's most beautiful stretches of coast, than about the glorious opportunities the Brasília project offered him as an architect. He cried out how hard it would be not to see his grandchild every day.

He has a horror of airplanes. The six hundred and fifty miles between Rio and Brasília will be a tough trek by car until the new road is finished. Once he tears himself away from Rio and settles in Brasília he seems to expect to stay there for the full two years. Did I think he'd be lonesome, he asked wistfully.

City Planner

Niemeyer would be the first to tell you that he considers it highly fitting that he will be working within the limits of Lucio Costa's city plan because he considers Lucio Costa more than any other man to be the inspirer and initiator of the modern movement in Brazilian architecture.

Lucio Costa shuns publicity and public statements as much as Niemeyer does. He is so selfeffacing that he sometimes avoids taking credit for his own work. All the public ever sees or hears of him is an occasional glimpse of his aquiline profile and bushy mustache lurking in the background of a photograph of some group of architects.

It was through Lucio Costa that this whole generation of Brazilian architects was brought into contact with the stimulating European work of the twenties. Coming from a family prominent in the government and in the armed services, he had the European upbringing of the wealthy Brazilians of the period before the wars. His father was a naval officer and eventually an admiral. Born in Toulon, Costa learned to read in London and attended a Swiss boarding school. The Europe he was brought up in teemed with revolutionary ideas in the arts.

Costa's attitude is that of the gifted amateur. As a boy he developed a taste for painting watercolors. In his teens he turned up in Rio to study design at the School of Fine Arts. There his interest in colonial architecture earned him the friendship of another talented and selfeffacing Brazilian, the Melo Franco de Andrade who devoted his life to the protection and restoration of Brazil's rich heritage of baroque architecture. It was as a restorer of ancient monuments that Lucio Costa first took up architectural work. His early house plans were in the neocolonial style.

When Le Corbusier, the French theorist of glass and steel construction, first visited Brazil in 1929, Lucio Costa had prepared the way for him. He had already been telling the young architects about his work and the work of Gropius and Frank Lloyd Wright and of the Italian futurists. They streamed out from the Frenchman's lectures dizzy with the "functional" use of the new materials: concrete and steel and tile and glass. Already a Polish settler named Warschavchik had been designing dwellings in "functional" concrete for wealthy business men in São Paulo. The new architecture took root.

By the time Le Corbusier returned to Brazil for a second visit a dozen talented young draftsmen were ready to call him master. Niemeyer had become Lucio Costa's intimate friend and collaborator. With Le Corbusier's advice the two of them launched their first great project: the Ministry of Education and Health in Rio.

Lucio Costa was the first chairman of the board that worked out the plans. Characteristically Costa retired in time to let the spotlight fall on his protégé Niemeyer as chief designer of that highly successful construction. Again when the Brazilian pavilion for the New York World's Fair in 1939 had to be designed, although Costa won the competition he claimed that Niemeyer's entry was better than his own and in the end the two men collaborated on the final plan.

The design which Kubitschek commissioned for Pampulha was Niemeyer's first job entirely on his own. He threw his cap over the windmill and developed a startlingly original style. Where Le Corbusier's and Lucio Costa's work had tended to straight lines and severe planes, Niemeyer was experimenting with the curves and swelling abstract forms of contemporary sculpture. When as President Kubitschek decided to stake his political future on the Brasília project he told Niemeyer he wanted him to design the new capital, all of it.

The Case Against

Like the wiseacres who raged against Belo Horizonte fifty years ago wellinformed people in Rio and São Paulo will prove to you with paper and pencil that the Brasília project is bound to fail. The Cariocas resent the loss of their capital. The whole scheme, they'll tell you, was cooked up to enrich the State of Minas Gerais and its politicians. A gigantic real estate speculation at the expense of the Brazilian economy. The city, they claim, will turn out another grandiose failure like the group of watertowers in decorative ironwork in the style of the Eiffel Tower a mayor of Belém in Pará bought at a Paris world's fair and set up in the center of the old tropical capital. From that day to this nobody has found any way to connect it to the city's water system.

They point out that the Pampulha project was a financial failure. A federal law against gambling put the casino out of business. Snails in the lake threatened the residents with schistosomiasis. The bishop refused to consecrate Niemeyer's gay little blue and white church. In the end a flood came which washed out the dam and left Niemeyer's famous yacht-club high and dry.

President Kubitschek's career, his opponents will tell you, has been littered with these unfinished enterprises. The municipal theater at Belo Horizonte was never completed. When Kubitschek left the governorship the building was invaded by squatters and became a slum. Brasília, editorial writers on the Rio newspapers were insisting, would turn out to be a desert favela on a colossal scale.

Why wasn't the money spent for schools to combat Brazil's seventy per cent illiteracy, or to start new industries or to stabilize finances, they ask. With the country swept by a ruinous inflation, they tell you, the last thing Brazil needs is the upkeep of a capital five hundred miles from nowhere.

Everything was being done backwards, they said. Instead of first building a presidential palace why didn't they spend the money on a new railroad? The steel girders that had to be bought in the States were unloaded at Rio, shipped up to Belo Horizonte on the regular gauge railroad, then transferred to the narrow gauge that took them to Anápolis. In Anápolis they were hoisted onto trucks and driven by road to Brasília. Many materials and even drums of gasoline were flown in by air.

The hotel is all very well, these critics said, but wouldn't it have been better to put the money into finishing the power plant and dam? Meanwhile electricity was being furnished by something like two hundred separate generators all using fuel oil or gasoline that had to be shipped seven hundred miles up from the coast.

In the summer of 1958 even people in favor of the transfer of the capital were claiming that time was against the project. The work couldn't be completed in two years. The dam alone would take three.

On the chosen date Brasília would be inaugurated as the capital in a ceremonial sense, to be sure, but when Dr. Kubitschek's term as President expired work would stop. His successor would certainly come from some other section of the country. No Brazilian politician liked to complete the work of any other politician. The new President would have other fish to fry. What buildings were already completed would remain as one more monument to the Brazilian mania for grandiose projects too hastily undertaken. Government workers and bureaucrats would continue to warm chairs in their offices in overcrowded Rio and to bask on its beautiful beaches. These sceptics were applying to the Brazilians the old adage that used to be applied to the Turks: always building, seldom finish, and never repair.

The Enthusiasm For

No matter how sceptical the Rio people may have been in the summer of 1958 about Brasília, the farmers and ranchers of the region seemed to believe in its future. At the Anápolis sales office for land in the new capital the agent said that although his office had only been open twenty days he had already sold fifty lots. The higher priced parcels went first. All the local business men seemed eager to invest. How many of them would build? Most of them, the agent thought. You got a fifteen per cent discount if you built in six months. At the Novacap office in Brasília the people in charge of sales seemed confident that eventually the sale of land would repay the cost of construction.

Brazilians plunge into real estate speculation with the enthusiasm of oldtime Floridians. The galloping inflation forces anyone who lays his hand on a few cruzeiros to invest the money in a piece of land or a house or a car or a radio rather than to see it lose buying power in a bank account. By the same token banks and corporations are driven continually to reinvest their funds.

Osorio, the young engineer from Belo Horizonte—recently graduated from the University of Miami—who drove us around in his jeep part of the time we were in Brasília, said he was already putting all he could save from his pay into a residential lot. Next he said he was planning to buy himself a piece of land within twenty or thirty miles of the capital and to plant it with eucalyptus trees. Eucalyptus would furnish a crop of timber every seven years. Everybody we met around Brasília, except the poor candongos who spent their money on drink and prostitutes down in the free city every payday, was investing in some phase of the enterprise. A sizable population was growing up with a stake in the completion of the city.

The augury most favorable to the success of Brasília lay, so it seemed to us, in the growth of Goiânia, a hundred and forty miles inland. Another invented city. Goiânia was designed a couple of decades ago by an architect named Attilio Lima. The plan was transferred right off the drafting board into the bush. When I was there on my way to visit Sayão's colônia ten years before the town's development had seemed completely stalled.

In 1958 we found Goiânia to be a flourishing city of fifty or sixty thousand people with paved treeshaded streets, an effective airport and several hotels, clean restaurants, hot and cold running water, and a great air of bustle and activity. Even streetcleaners. We saw them at work. Suburbs were springing up. The people in the stores looked wellfed and welldressed.

A middleclass city like some small agricultural capital in the North American midwest. No sign of the desperate rural poverty that we still found in the outskirts of Anápolis, even though that much older settlement had developed mightily as a milling and cheesemaking center.

The road to Anápolis to be sure had not been paved but a broad graded thoroughfare had taken the place of the old rutted trail wandering through the wilderness.

People told us that in central Brazil their economy didn't have the booms of the coffee country but that they didn't have the slumps either. Their products were upland rice and beans and wheat and cattle, all items in short supply in a nation that still had to import much of its food from abroad. They were independent of the export market. They were feeding Brazilians and getting rich on it. Already they were flying beef to Belém.

To a certain extent Goiás and Mato Grosso seemed to have prospered on the economic misfortunes of the coast. The inflation, the disastrous droughts in the northeasterly bulge, poverty and overcrowding in the coast cities were forcing people to move inland in search of a square meal. Ten years before whole families were on the move on foot and by ox-cart out into the agricultural colonies along the western river-valleys of Goiás. Now in 1958 the migration was mostly by truck. *Pau de arara* (parrot's perches) they called these jouncing trucks. They were true pioneers. They came buoyed up by the certainty that nothing they found in the new settlements could be worse than the poverty they had left behind.

A month before our visit to Brasília there had occurred what the directors of Novacap still spoke of as "the inundation." Fortyfive hundred people were unloaded from trucks almost overnight into the wilderness. They had heard about the new capital. They believed in Brasília. They wanted to settle there, so they arrived without asking leave of anybody.

The authorities at Novacap had plans drawn up to build what they called "satellite cities" to accommodate the population they knew would be attracted to the scene and to keep their capital city from becoming a rural slum before it was ever completed. They hadn't expected to need these plans so soon.

"We improvise," insists Dr. Pinheiro. In a few days they improvised a satellite city which they named Taguatinga.

Taguatinga was about twenty kilometers outside of the city limits of Brasília. To reach it we bounced over a rough road through a scrubby wilderness where an occasional rhea, the broadbilled South American ostrich, still loped among the termite nests. It certainly didn't look like a country where a man could live off the land.

It was exactly a month after the town's first settlement. We found hundreds of neat little houses ranged along recently staked out streets where watermains were already being laid. A pumping station had tapped what they claimed was an ample supply of water. Electric light was on its way. A moveable clinic in a whitepainted trailer furnished a firstaid station.

The mayor, a little old man dry and chipper as a cricket, turned out to have been a schoolmate of Dr. Pinheiro's at Ouro Prêto. He was chosen he told us, because he knew how to get along with working people. He showed us the blueprint of the city in a little office that smelt of raw boards.

Any settler could occupy a ten by thirty meter lot without down payment, but he had to build a house immediately and within a reasonable time to start paying the five hundred cruzeiros monthly which would earn him title in five years. That was less than four dollars according to the exchange of the time. Many of these refugees from the droughtstricken regions of eastern Brazil and from Bahia and from the baked out towns in the backlands of Minas seemed to have brought a little money with them, enough to buy some building materials. A good many of their houses were brick with tile roofs. Some had one brick wall and the rest of rough boards, to be replaced later, so their owners told us. Perhaps half the settlers lived in shelters of palmettoleaf thatch.

We found an air of cheerful bustle about everybody we met. Everything seemed new and fresh. Most of the people had put up their houses themselves. They were full of hopes and plans. On the main street bars and groceries were springing up. One shack claimed to be a nightclub. A man who said he'd been a stonemason back in Ceará proudly showed off his stock of canned goods and dried fruits and peanuts and a few drums of kerosene. Business wasn't too bad he said. That very day, so he told us, he'd made the first payment on his lot.

We were shown the parcel of land a French company had bought to set up a factory to make concrete culverts, the place where a brewery was about to move in, a small sawmill, a temporary laundry below the waterpump.

Beside a parked truck a priest was conducting an openair service. Little girls were waving palmfronds and singing. That's where the church was going to be.

We were introduced to a contractor. His two daughters were schoolteachers. They were going to improvise a school.

There was even a young man from Ceres, who'd moved away because things didn't move fast enough for him there. He owned a pickup truck. Everybody needed something hauled. He was doing a landoffice business. He was enthusiastic about his prospects. His friend was a housepainter. Everybody wanted something painted; more contracts than he'd ever imagined.

Most of the people worked in Brasília. A bus service was set up to take them back and forth. Their gripe was that the fare was too high. Otherwise they were delighted. They said they liked the upland air and the cool nights and the dry climate. Wages were better than they were accustomed to.

They were convinced that by the time they took title to their lots their land would be worth a great deal more than they paid for it.

When the settlers at Taguatinga spoke about Brasília, about the expense of going back and forth from Brasília, it was as if the city actually existed. For them it was already a metropolis. These immigrants were not worried about the problems of finance and the difficulties of transportation any more than our immigrants were a hundred years ago when they settled the western states. They had sold everything they owned and moved out here in the wilderness hundreds of miles from their homes because they believed in Brasília.

Dom Bosco's Dream

The evening before we went back to Rio we were standing beside Osorio's jeep in front of a pointed white shrine on the brow of a hill overgrown with scraggly trees and dotted with the red clay nests of the termites. Behind us lay miles of dry silent wilderness. This shrine was the first building they put up, Osorio explained, to commemorate the missionary friar who forecast a future civilization for these central highlands. Dom Bosco's statue looked out across a broad shadowy valley towards the streaks of dust that hung level in the evening air over the opposite ridge.

A faint roar came to us from the construction work. Draglines, bulldozers, sheepsfoot rollers, graders: earthmoving machines of every type were at work twentyfour hours a day leveling the summit of the long hogback which formed the center of Brazil's new capital.

On the horizon beyond, the red sun set in purple behind a smooth distant ridge. Osorio pointed out the white upside down arches of the palace and the pontoon shape of the hotel and the blocks of apartments shapeless under their scaffolding.

"Soon you'll see behind them the Triangle of the Three

Powers and the downtown district. You can imagine them already," he said, with a catch in his breath. "The neon lights will go on . . . You'll see them reflected in the lake."

He pointed out the location of the lot he had bought himself in the residential suburb across the lake from the city. The light scratches of a tractor trail around the flanks of the hills indicated where the lake level would be.

"You'll go to your office in a rowboat?" He corrected me. "By motorboat," he said.

A ragged grimy man with clearcut dark features stood looking intently up into Dom Bosco's face as he listened to our conversation.

"Ask him how he got here. It's miles from anywhere. Ours is the only car."

"He lives here," answered Osorio grinning. "He's a charcoal burner from Mato Grosso. He's cutting trees in all these valleys that will be flooded when they finish the dam."

There was no house in sight. Night was coming on fast. The valleys were drowned in dusk. In the tricky light of the last gloaming you could swear you could see the completed city, reflected into the lake from the opposite ridge. The streaks of blue mist might be the surface of the water.

The ragged man, as pleased as if he were pointing out a mansion, pointed out a tiny leanto way down on the valley floor. "That's my house," he said proudly.

"But it's at the bottom of the lake."

The idea seemed to please the ragged man. "Of course." He nodded delightedly. "I live at the bottom of the lake."

IV

THE RED DUST OF MARINGÁ

Monte Alegre

When you drive northwest from Curitiba, the capital of Paraná, through that state's beautiful midlands you come after four or five hours to a region densely forested with evergreens. What is known as the Paraná pine, a conifer which is really a kind of araucaria with a habit of growth resembling the umbrella pine of California, gives a special accent to the sharp hills and undulating valleys. In this region the piney forests cover hundreds of square miles. In the middle of them, taking advantage for water power of one of the swift green streams which flow towards the Paraná River to the westward, stands the Monte Alegre papermill.

Monte Alegre, with its guards and its gates and treeshaded streets and standardized stone houses around green lawns, looks like an oldfashioned company town in New England or eastern Canada. It is the headquarters of the Klabin Industries which furnish about a third of the newsprint used in São Paulo and Rio. This powerful group of companies constitutes a family enterprise very typical of Brazilian big business.

Three generations ago a Lithuanian immigrant opened a small stationery store in São Paulo. As his business increased he found it hard to keep his store supplied with paper. Shipments from Europe were irregular and unreliable. He started experimenting with making paper himself. Eventually he found himself operating the first successful papermill in Brazil. His sons turned out to be good businessmen. They imported European technicians, bought up vast tracts of virgin forest and built what was in its day a thoroughly uptodate papermill. So that they would be sure not to run out of pulpwood, they embarked on a treeplanting program to renew the forests of Paraná pine as fast as they cut them down. To use the byproducts they branched out into chemicals and plastics.

In Curitiba, a pleasantly literate city with a handsome public library and quite a background of publishing and historical research, I had met one of the grandsons of the original Klabin. I was there to give a talk at one of the binational centers which offer courses in the English language and library service and lectures on North American topics. While these centers were State Department enterprises, they had at that time considerable local backing, and some of them were said to be selfsupporting. In Curitiba it was amusing to discover that my audience was made up largely of German-speaking people. They came from German families that had been in Paraná for several generations. Some of them had never been in Germany. They told me that if I'd visit the neighboring state of Santa Catarina I would find the atmosphere even more Germanic. Horacio Klabin had heard I was interested in the mushrooming settlements of the hinterland, and handsomely offered to drive our little party out to visit his family enterprises around Monte Alegre. He had a new city of his own he wanted us to see.

On the drive out, over what was then a dirt road dusty and potholed from continual truck traffic, what struck us most was that so many of the settlers in the dilapidated roadside shacks were blueeyed and lighthaired. Towheaded children were everywhere. Klabin explained to us that these people sprang from a Polish immigration some twenty or thirty years before. Their language was Portuguese and their customs Brazilian. Most of them had forgotten the Polish language.

Horacio Klabin was a tall, dark, disenchanted man with a somewhat abstracted manner. His education and cultural formation seemed entirely European. He was up on all the latest developments in art and literature the world over. He evidently read Russian. He was painfully conscious of every development of Soviet expansion and wellinformed on the writers of the famous "thaw" that was then threatening the rigidity of Communist dogma. Dining at his house in Monte Alegre that night, we found the conversation international; we might have been at Fontainebleau or some Parisian suburb along the Marne.

He put us up at the company hotel. From the engineers and technicians and their wives and families passing through the lobby you could hear almost every European language; a United Nations, the Brazilians called it.

In the morning after walking through the huge papermill, we crossed the river to the development Horacio Klabin was promoting on his own on the green hillside facing the plant. His idea was to furnish homes that working people and technicians could buy on the installment plan, so as to get them out of the semifeudal atmosphere of the company town. Everything in the new city was to be independent of the papermill. White walls, red tiles, green louvers. Flowering shrubs, beautiful vegetation. There was an air of modest originality about these constructions. He showed us a variety of whitewalled residences of different sizes, tailored to the salaries of the people he wanted to see buy them. Four of the most attractive villas were set on a terrace that cut into the steep riverbank. A Frenchman owned one, a Hungarian another, a German a third. The last was occupied by the Brazilian salesagent for the real estate enterprise.

When Horacio Klabin showed us his nursery on the summit

of the hill, his manner took on real animation. This was his
hobby. He muttered deprecatingly that his whole family was
obsessed with planting trees. The trees he wanted to grow
at Monte Alegre were olives.

In colonial times the Brazilians were not allowed to plant
olive trees, so that olive oil should remain a Portuguese monopoly, he explained. Since independence nobody had thought
to try to grow olives on a large scale in Brazil. He had imported stock and seeds from Portugal and Spain and Italy
and the Near East. He had some California varieties. His
young trees were thriving. Soon they would bear. If he could
introduce an olive oil industry into central Paraná, he said
with his reserved smile, he really would have accomplished
something for his country.

Seven Year Old City

Next day he arranged for a small plane to take us further
to the north and west to the new town of Maringá.

The first thing we noticed as we circled for a landing over
the rawlooking airstrip was the red earth. Newly planted coffeetrees stretched in neatly checked rows in every direction,
uniform deepgreen balls. From the air the plantations looked
like a red checkerboard evenly set with green glassheaded pins.
There is a great deal of red earth in the interior of Brazil,
but this earth of Maringá was redder than red.

We had hardly a chance to stretch our legs, cramped from
the plane ride, before an eager young man strode up to us
with his hand out exclaiming that we were the guests of the
Northwest Paraná Development Company and that he was
going to show us the city of Maringá which seven years o'clock
was only forest primeval. Like many things in Maringá our
guide's English was new and rather hastily put together. He
had learned it out of a phrasebook. He would say "o'clock"
when he meant "ago." We got along famously all the same.

His cheerful enthusiasm made up for everything. As he ushered us into his car, which was deeply stained in red, he added that he could show us the forest primeval just as it had been seven years o'clock because a few acres had been left in their natural state for a public park.

The soil was perfect for coffee he told us. These new plantations just coming into bearing were proving profitable, but already the planters had to be looking around for new crops. They were all too conscious that they had to face a world surplus of coffee. Some were setting out longstaple cotton between the rows of coffeetrees. Others were turning to corn, and the brown beans which were the national staple, and soya and cattle. Texans from the King Ranch were crossing their famous Santa Gertrudis breed with the local zebu to find a type of cattle that suited the region exactly. The pastures were unbelievably lush. This was one of the richest bands of soil in the world. "Look at this soil," our friend scraped a little off the side of his jeep. "It will grow anything."

Maringá made us think of Mark Twain's and Bret Harte's Wild West of a hundred years ago, except that the pioneers rode jeeps instead of horses and arrived by plane instead of by stage coach. Everybody we talked to was full of bluesky speculations and slaphappy confidence. Our friend drove us through billowing clouds of red dust as he explained the layout of the city to be. It was like a Florida development in one of the great booms, only with a note of fantasy exclusively Brazilian.

We were shown residences and office buildings in the most original architectural styles, freshplanted parks, a jockey club for horse racing, a handsome tiled pool at the swimming club, and a children's playground with the most uptodate equipment.

The forest preserve was an incredibly beautiful stretch of primeval tropical woodland with a pond and a slathouse for growing orchids. A naturalist's dream. The place was full of birds and butterflies and grotesque tropical flowers. Up in the tops of the seventy foot trees there was a rustling that we were told was monkeys, but nothing would induce our small arboreal cousins to show their faces.

At lunch in the airconditioned restaurant of the scarcely finished hotel our friend explained that Maringá hadn't really made a start until seven years before. The city already had eight thousand inhabitants, with an estimated fifteen thousand in the environs, schools, a newspaper, a hospital, and twentytwo banks.

The development company he worked for began as a land-selling scheme. Thirty years before a British concern had obtained title to hundreds of square miles of the richest red-soil land in the world in northern Paraná and in the western part of the state of São Paulo. They had built a railroad and promoted Londrina, fifty miles nearer the city of São Paulo.

Now Londrina was a staid and established provincial city famous for its white skyscrapers, its treeshaded streets and handsome airport. The London company, in the sweeping liquidation of British holdings brought about by the second war, sold out to a Brazilian concern.

"Maringá is all Brazilian," cried our guide. "We have settlers from everywhere, from Minas and Ceará, refugees from the droughts cf the North East; from Santos and the gaucho country to the south." There were Greeks and Spaniards and Portuguese and Italians, refugees from the ironcurtain countries of Eastern Europe, and a few Japanese gardeners.

Since the land was almost all disposed of, the company had turned to producing and marketing agricultural products. Of course, our guide admitted, they had their difficulties. The roads were bad. The railroad service couldn't be worse. The state and national governments were far away. He brought his fist down on the table and burst out with the oft repeated adage: "Brazil grows at night when the politicians sleep . . . Eeneetiative!" He smiled broadly. "We do it ourselves."

Opposite the hotel we found them laying the foundations

for the cathedral of Maringá. Inside a little shed we saw the maquette. It was to be the tallest cathedral in South America, a concrete cone three hundred and seventytwo feet high, set on twelve pointed gables, one for each of the twelve apostles. It would cost thirty million cruzeiros. Already they had raised five million. Their bishop was a young man, very enterprising, our guide pointed out. He gave us a colossal wink. The bishop was promising the coffee planters five years without a frost if they put up the funds.

Old Maringá

We continued our tour. He drove us out into the outskirts to show us a row of ramshackle stores and a bar or two along a rutted road. They were frame buildings with clapboard false fronts all deeply coated with the cloying red dust.

"Like western cinema, not?" He made bang bang noises with appropriate gestures. We agreed it did look like the set for a Western. "This is old Maringá," he said in a tone of disgust, "builded ten years o'clock." He gave a snort. "Soon we tear down."

Inside the city the dust had been bad enough but in the outskirts you strangled in it. Our handkerchiefs were stained red from trying to wipe it off our sweaty faces. Our guide noticed that we were choking. We must not worry about the dust he told us consolingly. They had a doctor there, a very good doctor, who had discovered that the dust of Maringá was rich in terramycin. Maybe we had some infection; the dust of Maringá would cure it.

V

THROUGH BRAZIL'S BACK DOOR

From the Snowpeaks into Amazonas

In the summer of 1962 my wife and daughter and I took the jet flight from New York which landed us, long before we had become accustomed to the thought of arriving there, in Lima. After a couple of weeks amid the mystifications of Peruvian politics and the marvels of ancient textiles and sculptured ceramics in the Lima museums and the grandeur of the Stone Age architecture of the Andes, we are heading for Brazil.

Our plane left the old Faucett airport before dawn, circled over the dim city and the shrouded ocean and turned sharply into the daybreak. Now we are boring into the glare of the risen sun as we climb over the cocoacolored mountains that thrust up like islands through the cottony overcast which hangs eternally over the seaboard desert of the Pacific slope. No more vegetation on them than on the face of the moon. The first waters we see below us, thin trickles taking a northward course down the far slopes of the coastal cordillera, are already bound for the Amazon.

Except for some high thin cirrus the air is clear beyond the coastal range. The further mountains rear rock faces of upended strata, black organshapes in the shadow. Beyond, crystal sharp against a green horizon, tower the snowpeaks.

Between the heaving slopes of the second and third ranges the Urubamba River, tumbling northward in glassclear rapids out of the southern confines of Peru, drains the valleys and canyons which were the seat of the Andean civilizations. There we had walked panting among the earthquake-battered remnants of Spanish Cuzco which totter precariously on the unshakable foundations fitted together stone by stone by the ancient Indian builders. We had seen the huge citadel of Sacsahuamán squatting on the mountain above Cuzco and, in the valley beyond, Ollantaytambo's pyramid of ruins guarding its circus of green hills terraced in prehistoric days to the very summit. A few miles downstream we had scrambled around the stony masses of Machu Picchu, perched two thousand feet above the brawling river on a toothed height as steep as the mountains the Chinese painters imagined for their landscapes.

Two hundred miles north of Machu Picchu the Urubamba joins the Tambo to form the Ucayali which becomes navigable for river boats at Pucallpa. Already you can reach Pucallpa by truck or jeep or with luck by car from Lima. The Peruvians are pushing through a paved road from the coast to Pucallpa and its Brazilian extension is already groping its way through the wilderness of the new state of Acre to reach Pôrto Velho on the Madeira River six hundred miles to the east.

From Pucallpa barges and small river boats take five or six days to reach Iquitos. Iquitos, still in Peru, twentythree hundred miles from the Atlantic, is head of navigation for oceangoing steamers on the Amazon. From the junction of the Ucayali with Rio Marañón some fifty miles from Iquitos the Peruvians call the great river the Amazon, but the Brazilians insist that it is the Rio Solimoes until, more than a thousand miles downstream, it joins the Rio Negro below Manaus.

A Rainforest Economy

The only practical way of reaching Iquitos is by air. The head of ocean navigation of the Amazon is still an island inaccessible by road. After flitting between the jagged snowteeth of the highest Andes the plane starts to toboggan downward through the massed cumulus clouds that steam up incessantly from the rainy eastern slopes.

After rumbling for a long time amid a churn of mist we begin to see trees through rents in the clouds. The wooded slopes below us heave in ridges cut by swift straight streams occasionally barred by the white spume of rapids. As the hills subside the rivers seem for a while to strangle in the rainforest.

Now we are flying low over what seems a mossy plain, only the tendrils of the moss are gigantic trees. The rivers have broken through below us, muddy and turgid now, and flow in restless curves from oxbow to oxbow. As far as you can see in every direction the forest is cut by the meanderings and the arabesques of rampaging rivers.

We are looking down on an unending struggle between the weight of the hurrying water and the fibrous density of the treepacked land. This titanic wrestling match has left the jungle scarred by the scratches of old riverbeds as if by the claws of some vast jaguar. The rivers slither like great snakes between the tottering trees, leaving their castoff courses to one side or the other in lagoons and sickleshaped backwaters. In some places the subsiding waters have left reedy ponds or palegreen savannas. Every shape you see results from the war between land and water. There's still not a sign of human occupation. Not a canoe, not a hut, not a smoke.

We are headed east flying low above the olivegreen coils of the Rio Marañon when, along the broadly curving silty beaches, a different green appears which could be rice that human hands have sown. A log half pulled up on a beach might be a dugout. A pile of dry palm leaves might be a thatched hut. There is smoke from brush fires.

Now there is an unmistakable canoe, the flash of the paddle of a man paddling in the bow. A long thatched object moving upstream must be a motorboat. There's a road below with toy trucks, tin roofs, tiled roofs under palms, a beach hatched with rows of dugouts, a wide stretch of river full of canoes and launches; and the plane is spiraling down into the airfield.

Iquitos turns out to be two towns. There's the outpost Peruvian city: a gridiron of streets of stone and rubble houses, stores, banks, a motion picture theater, markets, a hotel on a bluff overlooking the river run by the Peruvian Government to encourage tourists; and then there's the Amazonian river town. This they call the port of Belén.

In the port everything is afloat. Houses, built of poles and thatch tied together with jungle vines, are set on rafts made of great logs of various light woods similar to balsawood. At high water the whole settlement would be afloat in the river but the waters in the upper Amazon basin are low now (mid-August), so half the riverport is stranded on the brown beach.

The houses stretch for half a mile in straggling rows. On the hump of the great sand bar are thatched shops selling groceries and drygoods, bars, small restaurants. The river merchants buy snakeskins, pelts, and alligator hides, bananas, rice. At the entrance to one thatched hut is a crate of orange and brown small monkeys. Their tiny black faces peer out wretchedly through the slats. From another door a big black terrapin is just about to make good his escape when he's recaptured and turned ignominiously over on his back.

There are pet parrots and parakeets everywhere. Pigs and small children roam in the alleys. A dead iguana rots in a puddle at the river's edge. Black buzzards perch on the rooftrees.

It is hot. The place smells, but now and then a gust of freshness comes from the river. The people are quiet and friendly and go about their business with an air of great good-nature. Nobody stares at a stranger.

These are not exactly Peruvians or Brazilians. They are river people of the Amazon, made up perhaps two thirds of forest Indian, a third of various brownskinned Mediterranean strains with a touch of Negro. They are darker than the Indians of the forest tribes.

The river is full of coming and going in dugout canoes, or in enlarged dugouts driven by an outboard motor where the passengers sit comfortably under a light thatch of palm leaves. There are motorboats and launches in all sorts of homemade shapes. Women are arriving from little hamlets up and down stream in their brightest clothes to market and to buy and sell. The man paddling is always in the bow. Often the woman in the stern has a pink or red sunshade.

On the bank, and from the rafts the houses float on, women are washing clothes. Brown children are bathing. One stark naked little girl, modestly hidden from view by an enormous straw hat bigger than she is, is dunking herself between her home and the muddy shore.

Further out men fish from canoes, using fishspears or throwing a round casting net. An occasional old man bottom-fishes with a bamboo pole. Fish are plentiful we are told because the water is low. Among the canoes dolphins occasionally surface, the famous pink porpoises of the Amazon. Some are pinkish, some light gray, some black. A boy tells us that the black ones are dangerous. They have been known to attack a canoe.

Iquitos proper—some people told us it had fifty thousand, others eighty thousand inhabitants—has considerable business in spite of the lack of overland links to the rest of the world. Everything that doesn't come by air has to come by river. The manager of one of the three Bata shoestores told us that he found it more economical to fly in his shoes from the factory in Callao. This was because of the pilfering that went on during the long truck and boat haul via Pucallpa.

Gasoline is cheap and plentiful as the crude oil comes down river from the Peruvian fields in the upper Marañon to a distillery a few miles below Iquitos. There's a plant for processing chicle brought in from the forest, an alcohol distillery and a sawmill for tropical woods.

The docks and warehouses for oceangoing steamers, mostly monthly ships of the Booth Line out of Liverpool, are new and modern. The channel is reported to have ample depth for ships drawing fourteen feet. The city is the furnishing center for a huge region of the upper Amazon basin reaching to the Ecuadorian and Colombian borders. Protected by chloroquin from malaria and by the vaccine from jungle yellow fever, with the help of outboard motors the mestizo watermen and half civilized Indians are pushing up the rivers of the upper Amazon basin in all directions. They are fast annihilating the wild life.

Shrunken heads are a thing of the past. The few smuggled with great pretense of secrecy to gullible tourists are mostly dried monkey skulls.

Science's insatiable demand for small primates is depleting the monkey tribes. One dealer, a young man who started a number of years ago with a hundred *soles* for capital, and is now reputed to be a millionaire, told us how his hunters caught the poor banderlog. They pick a tree frequented by bands of small monkeys and hang ripe bananas in the branches to attract them. Gradually they get the monkeys accustomed to eating their bananas on the ground and then they set out pans of sweetened *aguardiente* among the bananas. The monkeys take to drinking it. The bands of drunken monkeys, the dealer told us, were irresistibly comic. Imagine a drunken monkey trying to peel a banana. When they are so drunk they can't climb, the hunters rush in and thrust them by the hundreds into burlap bags.

The large monkeys that roam in family groups have a grimmer fate. Since a shotgun would scare them, the hunters still use the Indian *pucuna* (*serebatana* is the Spanish and Portuguese name). The blowgun is a remarkably deadly weapon, shooting a tiny dart poisoned with curare with great force and accuracy at short range. The hunters shoot an old male, who is usually carrying a baby monkey on his back, and bag the rest of them when they crowd around to try to carry off the corpse. So that the monkeys can't pull the darts out in time the head of the dart is cut so that it breaks off under the skin. Curare kills even a large animal like a jaguar or tapir, we were told, in less than ten seconds.

There are seven firms in Iquitos exporting wild animals and tropical fish direct to the States. Tropical fish are the money makers. A rare specimen will bring a thousand soles. The story goes that there are more varieties of fish in the Amazon region than in all the other fresh waters of the world put together.

The trader equips the fishermen with boat and outboard and nets. When they bring in the fish he keeps them alive in tanks feeding them on tiny leeches which he breeds for the purpose until they can be sorted and counted. An expert waterman will count and sort forty thousand in an hour. Fungus diseases are the worst enemy.

The fish are shipped in plastic bags packed in cartons. Some of the spiny catfish types and the savage piranha have to be dosed with tranquilizers before they are packed so that they won't tear their plastic bags to pieces en route. A weekly plane from Miami picks up the shipments of fish and forest animals for sale to pet shops and laboratories. Recently shipments have started direct to Hamburg, Germany.

The tropical fish dealer told us that his main difficulty was keeping his fishermen at work. An independent lot. The most skillful only needed to work for him two or three times a year to keep going. When they made a few hundred dollars they would knock off and drink *pisco* and collect women until their money was all gone. The tribal Indians are monogamous. In most tribes only the *curaca* (chief) is allowed more than one wife; but the half-breed watermen pride themselves on the number of women they can keep. The trader told of a man with a plantation way up one of the tributary rivers, who kept seventeen. Each has her appointed job, fishing, tending manioc plantings, cooking, weaving mats or hammocks, making pottery. A happy family, the trader called them.

Iquitos has a budding tourist trade. A very blond German named Herman Becker has a camp on the Rio Mamón a few miles out of town and arranges trips out into the rainforest. His brighteyed Portuguese wife is an enthusiast for life *al aire libre*. Cruising in the fresh breeze up the endlessly winding rivers, seated under an umbrella in an outboard-driven dugout canoe is one of the pleasantest ways of traveling imaginable.

Becker's camp is full of local pet animals. It's like *The Swiss Family Robinson*. None of them are in cages. They seem to stay around because they like it. There is a kinkajou, several monkeys—one of them looks like a black Winston Churchill—parrots and macaws, a toucan, and a trompetero. The trompetero is a businesslike walking bird who eats ants and insects and joins the party when Mr. Becker's tourists walk through the jungle trails and to visit the half Indian settlements around about.

Roque, a Yagua boy whose grandfather was the tribal medicine man, walks ahead with a machete. Poor Roque, much against his will, has to put on his grass skirt and headdress when he shows off his skill with the blowgun for the visitors. When he is allowed to get back into his shirt and pants—

like people—you can see the satisfaction stand out all over him. He leads the way through the forest path hacking at the underbrush with his machete.

This is a Saturday. In the first palmleaf shelter we visit the man of the family is asleep dead drunk on the floor. His hairless face wears an expression of innocent satisfaction. It is explained that there has been some sort of fiesta. His women and children peer out sleepily from the shadows of the hut.

In the next set of huts a tall man with an aquiline nose rises to greet us. With a dignified gesture he invites us to sit on a bench under his thatch. He offers bananas. He's somewhat oddly dressed. He wears what looks like a woman's boudoir cap on his curly gray head and an assortment of blazerlike garments over a weird striped shirt. A man of means. There's an outboard motor in the yard and a shiny new piano accordion on one of the beds. A bottle of Italian vermouth stands among grimy glasses on the table. Mrs. Becker explains that he's the best hunter in the region, the father of twentyfour children out of two wives. His womenfolk raise guineapigs in a little corral. We pass the time of day with him in formal Spanish.

In other huts scattered under the trees we find the women working on pottery. Since they have no wheel even the largest pots are built up by hand out of long snakes of kneaded clay coiled in a spiral. Firing them on the embers without an oven is long and tedious and highly expert work. Then they are painted with handsome geometric designs and glazed and fired again. "Lazy things," says Mrs. Becker, "they'll only work when they feel like it."

A bonanza came to this whole part-Indian, part-halfbreed settlement a few nights ago when a herd of peccary swam the river and invaded their manioc plantation. The villagers turned out with clubs and guns and killed fiftysix. That means fresh and smoked meat for weeks. They proudly show us the skins—which bring a good price in Iquitos—stretched and salted for drying and several peccary shoats they captured for pets.

This happygolucky life is not without a certain enchantment. In another hut we find a group of men celebrating over a bottle of some kind of rotgut. More European blood here. You can tell by the stubbly beards. They swarm about us to offer us drinks. The stuff in the bottle smells like wood alcohol. We refuse as politely as possible. It's already dusk and they really are too drunk.

The man with the bottle latches onto my arm. "Doctor, you must have a drink"—in these parts anybody who can read and write is addressed as Doctor—"Mr. Engineer," he pleads, "please take a drink with us." How can a man refuse?

One gulp does it. We break away and hurry down the slippery riverbank to the waiting canoe.

The Photographer's Redskins

The other tourist entrepreneur is the local photographer, a genial and hospitable gentleman named Antonio Wong, who set up a hunting camp on the Rio Manaté, some fifty miles downstream from Iquitos, years ago before tourists were dreamed of, for his own pleasure, so he tells us. An enthusiastic hunter, he never hunts without a couple of Yagua Indians to find him the game. He whisks us downstream in a speedboat.

After lunch at his thatched and mosquito-netted camp set high on stilts on the bank of a narrow winding tributary river, we visit his private tribe of Indians. A large launch load of French tourists has come in ahead of us. The Indians—Yaguas of Mr. Wong's pet tribe—have come down specially from their settlement three and a half hours' walk back in the forest. They have dressed in their best grass skirts and grass headdresses to be shown off to the tourists. After the French depart Mr. Wong has us distribute cigarettes to the men and marshmallow candies to the ladies. He makes each of us hand out one item to each member of the tribe. In return the Indians present us with the little crowns of palm leaves they are wearing on their heads.

They are lightolive healthylooking people with mellow brown eyes. Their faces are daubed with ochre. Only a few of the women and children have the puffed-up bellies that come from eating too much cassava. They seem to be enormously amused by the tourists. Though they can't understand Spanish they laugh and laugh at the slightest thing anyone says. Perhaps it's embarrassment but more likely it is frank entertainment at the strange creatures that have appeared from the outer world. We get to laughing too. We look into each other's faces and laugh and laugh.

The curaca is a very young man but the witch doctor is old with a crinkled parchment skin. He stands hesitantly off by himself as if he weren't quite sure what his attitude should be.

After a while a flute and drum start playing a simple but not at all outlandish little tune and Mr. Wong and the oldest of the women, an old lady with numbers of rubber tires round her waist, dance a sort of twostep with incredible solemnity. It's a sight worth coming three thousand miles to see.

A Swiss gentleman has been bringing the house down by giving extra cigarettes to the Indians who have traces of whiskers. This proves an enormous joke because it's well-known that the forest Indians have very little hair on their bodies. Everybody roars. After giggling with them for a while more in their palmleaf shelter set high on stilts, where the women are smoking a few fish over a smoldering fire, we part amid fresh gales of laughter and return to our speedboat.

How come, we ask Mr. Wong, when we have him alone, that some of the Yagua women have permanent waves? Mr.

Wong explains with a show of annoyance that it's these Syrian traders. The Turkos, as they are known, scour the rivers in motorboats buying wild animal and reptile skins. To avoid paying in money they give the Indian women permanents in return for valuable pelts. Disgusting, says Mr. Wong.

Flight Downriver

From Iquitos to Manaus there's only one flight a week. The plane is a Catalina flying boat of the amphibian type known to the U. S. Navy in the Pacific war as a P.B.Y. Most of the sixteen seats are already taken so we have to crawl through the narrow waist to places scrunched up against the radio man's little table. Wicker seats have been set in the hull but otherwise very little has been done for the comfort of the passengers. There's a reek of gasoline. The only ventilation comes when the pilots open their side windows.

The seaplane rattles like a truckload of scrap as it takes off. We fly out over the river and cut across its windings in the early haze. The mist rises from the great trees in thin wisps like cotton batting twisted between thumb and forefinger. We cruise at a couple of thousand feet above the rainforest. In every direction the treetops stretch to the horizon.

Things are pleasantly informal aboard. The prettily gotten up Brazilian girl in the front seat must be the pilot's ladyfriend because before long she is sitting on his lap. So that the other passengers shan't feel neglected he invites us in rotation to climb into the copilot's seat where the air is fresh and the view magnificent. The steward, crawling among the packages that obstruct the seaplane's narrow waist, keeps plying us with gummy sandwiches and sicksweet *guaraná*. Guaraná, which can be quite good, is the national soft drink of Brazil. The Peruvian lady sitting next to my wife asks her if she minds the smell of the package she holds on her lap: it is fresh turtle meat she is carrying to a friend in Manaus.

After a couple of hours we were trundling down the landing strip at Letícia. Having dim memories of a noisy border dispute years ago between Brazil, Colombia, and Peru, which was settled, if I remember right, by Rondón's border commission awarding the place to Peru, I expected to find frontier guards, customs officers, and the like. There must be a village, but we saw no sign of it. We found the tiny new airport completely deserted except for a large crate of green parakeets. Inside were cartons and cartons full of plastic bags of tropical fish waiting for shipment. Out back a single dilapidated stationwagon stood waiting on the rutted road that wound off into the jungle.

Letícia is situated on the north bank of the Peruvian Amazon near the point where the borders of the three republics meet. If there were any internal trade between them the place should be an important riverport. Outside of the freight carried overseas by the Booth Line boats from Iquitos, the only largescale shipments we could hear of in these upper reaches of the river were the bargeloads of crude oil that go down from the Peruvian oilfields to the Brazilian government refinery near Manaus. The young man who managed one of the Bata shoestores in Iquitos had recently made a trip downstream to try to arrange some way of selling his product in the Brazilian settlements. He had come back discouraged. Bureaucratic complications made it impossible.

At Benjamin Constant, named for the Brazilian positivist who, as one of Pedro II's ministers, helped negotiate his abdication and became known to history as the father of the republic, we alight on the sleek brown surface of a river. This is the first Brazilian outpost, on the Rio Yavarí just above its junction with the main stream of the Amazon. The seaplane is pulled in to a landing by hawsers and a Negro boy and a white boy start working a twohanded pump to suck the gasoline out of drums scattered on the steep sticky clay bank.

While we are lounging around the float in the punishing sun, waiting for the boys to pump the tanks full, we find ourselves looking into a canoe which contains an unmistakably American portable refrigerator, a picnic basket with a thermos, a little blond boy in jumper and shorts, and a young American couple in straw hats. Just the group you would see in a national park in the States. Before we have a chance to attract their attention the man has started the outboard and they go gliding away up the river.

Later we learned that these were missionaries who had started a school, just the two of them, to teach reading and writing and some simple hygiene to the river dwellers, and that the fame of their school had spread far and wide.

On the takeoff the water roars about the hull, and surges olivecolored over the ports. The old amphibian, shaking and creaking, hitches itself above the treetops. The treetops spread to the horizon in every direction. As we soar, from the co-pilot's seat we can look out over the forest for ten, twenty, fifty, a hundred miles. Beyond those miles the same rivers the same treetops spread for a thousand miles to the north, to the south, to the west, and eastward for two thousand and more. The trees hide tiny settlements. In the open stretches of water between them you might see fishermen in canoes, or a lost gunboat with washing hung out to dry on the forward deck, showing the flag that flaunts the sovereignty of one of the three sovereign states. Hunters and fishermen, a few families collecting fruits and nuts, logging crews, now and then a sawmill. Thatched huts of halfbreeds who collect chicle and latex. The Weeping Wood, the romancers called it, the Green Hell. Outside of Antarctica it is the largest extension of terrain in the world that the human race has left unoccupied.

After Benjamin Constant the Catalina skims downstream, often following the river for many miles. We stop at occasional collections of thatched huts. At each stop the shape of the canoes that come alongside is a little different and the heartshaped paddles have a different design. The birds change; in some places herons predominate, in others flocks of small white gulls. Only the buzzards remain the same and the big cheerful yellowbellied bird you find all over Brazil, named from his call, *Bem-ti-ví-* (I see you). At one stop the only passenger to come aboard, along with a tiny package of mail, is a large scarlet macaw consigned to Manaus.

As we fly east the fine morning turns into a murky noon. It's bumpy going amid the boiling clouds. Whenever there's an opening below, a new river seems to be joining the main stream. Never the glimpse of a steamboat. Even canoes are rare. You can't tell which is the main river among the many parallel channels boiling through the coppery glare. Below everything is hurrying water, dark islands seen through slanting stripes of rain, a flash of silver beyond a dark elbow of densepacked trees, a bilious khakitinted channel' where some muddy confluent has poured in. A landscape like Gustave Doré's dreams of hell.

At last we break out of the overcast and glide through sunlight over the lake of Tefé. The water is the color of clear weak coffee. The town of Tefé has an oddly civilized look, with one small row of houses that might be on the banks of the Seine. The air is clear as the water. The sky is full of gulls. There's a cool breeze blowing. The passengers troop up the steep duckboards to the local boardinghouse where lunch is laid out on long tables. Turkey and rice and black beans and baked bananas all sprinkled with cassava flour. At the grocery next door you can buy cold beer.

From Tefé to Manaus is four long hours through turbulent clouds. In spite of cotton stuffed in our ears the motors are deafening. Legs are cramped. By the time the old Catalina goes slambanging down the runway at the Manaus airport the sudden night of the tropics is closing down.

Haunted City

Manaus, the capital of the vastest and least populated of the states that make up the Brazilian union, climbs a group of hills behind a bluff some ten miles above the junction of the Rio Negro with the Rio Solimoes to form the oceanlike flood of muddy fresh water the Brazilians call the Rio Mar, their Amazon. It is a city beset with nostalgia.

The opera house on the hill, now restored to all its gaudy splendor, testifies not only to the exuberant bad taste of the late nineteenth century but to a certain enthusiasm of the grand era of capitalist promotion which can never be recaptured. The fortunes of the rubber barons who put up the money to build it have long since been spent and forgotten, but ghosts of old bonanzas linger in the fetid streets which lead up to the wide square the building fronts on, which is paved in wavy mosaic like the famous Rocio in Lisbon.

The enormous steel pontoons of the floating wharves so ingeniously arranged to rise and fall with the stages of the Rio Negro are monuments not only to the nineteenth century's engineering skill, but also to its faith in the inevitable benefits of world commerce linking the nations. The crowding steamers from every European port that kept the central conveyor railroad so busy sank to the bottom during the First World War and were never replaced, but impressive traces of steamship offices and freight agencies still remain in the downtown buildings.

The wide ruined avenues with their broken pavements, dark at night because there is not enough electric power to light them, the scarfaced public buildings designed at the Paris Beaux-Arts, the neglected parks where rampant trees have invaded the footpaths, the dilapidated European trolley-cars, the empty aviary and the gay little clock tower that's lost its clock in the waterfront square which is the center of the city's traffic, all still echo memories of mighty projects that have failed.

Manaus is haunted by every feverish dream that has flitted through the shadows of this most enormous of the world's rainforests ever since Orellana, more than four hundred years ago, after straying away from one of Pizarro's expeditions, made his first desperate journey downriver. On the heels of the slavers and the prospectors for diamonds and the placerminers for gold came the *seringueiros*: the exploitation and the peonage and the quick riches of the great rubber boom. *Borracha* is still a word to conjure with.

An Englishman named Henry Wickham, whose name is a hissing among the riversettlements, smuggled seeds of *Hevea brasiliensis*, the wild rubber tree, out to the Malay States. Intelligent selection produced improved varieties and Amazonia lost its monopoly of the world market. The exploitation of Amazonian rubber strangled in its own ineptitude. Cultivated rubber soon proved it could outsell the wild product even in its home port. The production of synthetics, spurred on by the exigencies of the Second World War, relegated the natural product to a still more subsidiary position; but today an increasing demand, resulting from inordinately increased production in the automotive and electrical goods industries, has opened a new market for various natural rubber, latex, and gutta-percha products.

The challenge of Amazon rubber appealed to Henry Ford's imagination. He was bound he'd find a way to cultivate the rubber tree in its natural home, but his carefully planned and segregated settlements; Fordlândia, and Belterra on the Rio Tapajós, have hardly left any more trace than the huts of the slaphappy seringueiros who plodded through the forests gathering the "tears" of the wild rubbertrees.

Ford's was only one of a hundred projects that the jungle-vines have overgrown. The vast effort expended in the construction of the Madeira-Mamoré Railroad, which was to link Amazonas with Bolivia and the Pacific coast, though trains do occasionally run on it, has left little behind except legend. Stories of failure in face of the rainforest hang about every streetcorner in Manaus. The city's history is of great plans gone awry. Even the building of the new airconditioned hotel, which was to have brought in the benefits of the international tourist trade, ended in the bankruptcy of the promoter. Already the new hotel wears the air of having seen better days.

Projects . . . Projects

In the bar and in the patio of the Hotel Amazonas, cooled by the forced draft from a large ventilating fan, men sit in their shirtsleeves and talk excitedly of the great future of the state of Amazonas. The old bogeys of malaria and yellow fever have been driven back up into the most distant tributaries. Hygiene will do the rest.

Some airline should buy this hotel and renovate it and channel the flow of tourists with money to spend into sport-fishing on the rivers, and exploration, so easy with proper motorboats, of the watery wilderness.

They rattle off lists of minerals and their locations: gold, nickel, hematite, manganese, tin, bauxite, tungsten. Companies are promoting the cultivation of the Brazil nut and the palms and other trees that produce vegetable oils. There are said to be a hundred and nineteen varieties susceptible of exploitation.

Agronomists are catching fire at the first rumors of a technical breakthrough on the production of fertilizers suitable for the special conditions of the tropical rainforest. Locked in certain crumbling formations of rock in the worndown mountain ranges of eastern Brazil there is said to be enough available minerals in a substance called biotite to revolutionize tropical agriculture. In northern Australia the experiment stations are turning under a nitrogenproducing plant named *Indigofera* that may solve the problem of nitrogen.

Agricultural colonies have been successful in the river valleys of Mato Grosso and Goiás. Why not turn the surplus population of the barren northeast into Amazonas? With proper farming and public health the merest corner of Amazonas could support a population equal to the present population of the entire nation.

While they talk they eat toasted Brazil nuts. Nothing better. Why not can them and ship them to New York and make a fortune?

The city of Manaus, when you walk around by day, does show a few signs of new construction. A new electric light plant, which is to operate on crude oil brought in from Venezuela and Peru, is about to go into operation to furnish muchneeded power and even light for the city streets.

The explanation of why this plant had to be bought entire was not without interest. A good deal of the component machinery could have been manufactured in Brazil, but the result of the laws passed by the federal congress seeking to insure the use of Brazilmade products was that if any item were bought in Brazil the whole inventory of things that had to be bought abroad: generators, various sorts of piping and tubing, copper wire and all the rest, would have had to be approved item by item by the interested government bureaus. Every purchase would be endlessly obstructed by the appropriate bureaucrats. The result would have been interminable delay. To buy an entire plant abroad only one authorization was necessary. A neat case of selfdefeating legislation.

A thoroughly uptodate factory newly installed produces laminated veneer woods. There German and Czechoslovakian

machinery is powered by American furnaces. A nearby jute-
mill has just doubled its capacity. Each of these projects has
brought in a group of foreign engineers to supervise the new
installations. There aren't enough Brazilian engineers, and
those who are competent would rather work in the cosmopolitan regions of Rio and São Paulo. In spite of themselves
the imported engineers catch the speculative fever.

A tall young Hungarian working on the generators at the
electric light plant could talk of nothing but the bauxite and
manganese he's found on his wife's ranch in Amapá at the
northern mouth of the Amazon and his vast catches of fish,
trolling up the Rio Negro north of Manaus, every afternoon
after work.

The pleasantest part of Manaus is a region of gardens and
candycolored villas which rambles among the hills that rise
behind the old town. In these latitudes even the elevation of
a couple of hundred feet above the river brings a noticeable
freshness to the air. A new hardtop road extends between
gardens, plantations of pineapple and sugarcane and shady
mango groves, out into the sandy redsoiled uplands.

Since it's a fine Sunday morning the road is full of small
cars and families on bicycles or on foot headed out for the
picnic grounds and swimming holes improvised wherever the
road crosses a clear stream. Every rustcolored sandy beach is
full of bathers, brown amid the vivid greens of mangoes and
banana trees. We pass a nightclub where roulettewheels, supposed to be illegal in Brazil, spin undisturbed by the local
authorities.

After the baths and the resorts, the road cuts through rolling
hills planted with experimental groves of rubber trees grafted
with new varieties imported from Africa and the Far East.
Here, we are told, the present state governor, still hopeful in
the face of the failure of the largescale experiments of the

Ford Company years ago, is promoting a fresh effort to put Amazon rubber cultivation on a commercial basis.

Beyond the rubber plantations the homesteaders begin. Wherever a new road opens in Brazil a band of settlement spreads out along it. Here settlers are encouraged to build themselves houses and to clear small farms on six and a half acre tracts with a good wide frontage on the road. If the planting meets the requirements the settlers are supposed to get title to the land with the lapse of a year.

Clearing land in these parts is a rough business. We heard the same story from Iquitos on. Everything favors the growth of trees over other types of vegetation. Clearing a small patch is long and tedious, even with a bulldozer. It is doubtful whether it is worth the effort and expense. If, as in most cases, a man has only his own two arms and an axe and machete, about the best he can do is burn the underbrush and let the big trees lie where they fall. Grubbing with his machete or a long brushhook he'll plant corn or manioc in the scorched loam. Chemical fertilizers are unobtainable and even if they could be had the types used in regions of moderate rainfall would wash away with the first tropical downpour. Often, after the tremendous labor of clearing, the patch will only yield one crop because whatever plantfoods there were in the soil will have been dissipated by the continual rains. The procedure is to let the land grow up after harvesting and to go to work to make another clearing.

The region we are going through this morning has, for Amazonas, better than average soil and a better than average climate. We find ourselves passing some flourishing plantations of corn, papaya and of the inevitable bushy manioc with its fivefingered redtinted leaves.

We notice a bristlebearded man walking out with a firm step down the center of the road. He wears a battered slouch hat. His clothes, all rags, are stained with the red color of the land. A long shotgun is slung over his shoulder. He makes no move to get out of the way of the car. It's the car that has to swerve to get around him. "He's a hunter," says the stout citybred man who owns the car. "No struggling with unfriendly vegetation for him. He'll shoot the animals and pick the wild fruits." There's a touch of awed admiration in his voice. "For weeks he'll stay out in the forest alone, hunting game . . . The forest is his home."

The surprise of the morning was when, in an open lot fringed with palms, we came upon a group of boys playing baseball. The ballplayers were the first sign we saw of a colony of fifty or sixty Japanese families settled here during the last three years. They have organized a cooperative under the management of a Japanese agronomist to grow black pepper. We began to see carefully weeded rows of staked pepper vines. The palmthatched huts began to take on an indefinable Japanese look. Men wearing conical straw hats were pushing light carts rigged with bicycle wheels. Each house had a vegetable patch and an occasional flowering vine.

The settlers' houses, built on a framework of poles, lashed together in the local manner by jungle vines, and roofed and walled with palmleaf thatch, were hardly more than shelters against the rain and the sun, but a great neatness prevailed inside. Their tables and benches were hewn out of the local woods.

Everybody had a transistor radio. Their few utensils were cheap imports but shining clean. The kitchens had white enameled gas ranges fired by bottled propane gas trucked out from Manaus. The women were all smiles when we noticed how new they were.

A young man walked us around the cleantilled pepper vines. They grow on heavy stakes like polebeans. The foliage has a darker, glossier look. Once they start to bloom they keep on bearing the racemes of green shotlike peppers for a number of years. When we asked about fertilizers our friend answered with a certain embarrassmet that all they could get was the hulls of the *castanha* or Brazil nut, sold by the small factories that shell and pack the meats of this most characteristic of Amazonian products. Not much good but it was all that could be had.

When we were about to leave the Japanese picked a couple of the fragrant yellow melonlike fruits of the passionflower vine and insisted on our taking them as a present.

We were shown their school. The school is named for Ryoto Oyama.

Ryoto Oyama was the Japanese who, acting as a sort of opposite number to Henry Wickham, smuggled seed of the jute plant out of Bengal and introduced it in Brazil. Jute is now one of the principal crops of the region. The Japanese are popular in Amazonas.

Back in Manaus, at the exhibit put on by the Association of Commerce, the face of the man in charge lights up when I ask him about jute. The dollar value of jute as a cash crop is fast catching up with all the wild rubber, latex, and gutta-percha products combined. Brazil nuts, veneer woods, vegetable oils, tropical fruits, pepper and guaraná roots and berries (the basis of the Brazilian soft drink), fish and chicle; he rattles off the export products.

Petroleum . . . he frowns when the word comes up.

He tells us that Petrobras, the Brazilian government corporation in charge of the oil industry, has two hundred and fifty prospectors in the field looking for oil. Nothing. He has been told that no results are to be expected till 1966. Meanwhile the local distillery has to depend on Peru and Venezuela and on an occasional shipment from the fardistant Brazilian field at Bahia.

Now jute. He is smiling again. It is suited to the soil. It is easy to cultivate and to process. The growing of jute will give Amazonas a breathing space while the exploitation of other products is being developed.

Like Iquitos, Manaus consists of two towns, the muscle-bound old city on its hills and a floating town which is the buying and selling center for the dwellers on the rivers and creeks for miles upstream and downstream. Fifty thousand people are said to live on the *flutuantes,* as they call the floating houses around Manaus. Since the stages of the river have a different schedule here than in the Peruvian region a thousand miles upstream, the water is high now. The rafts are all afloat.

A large bay downstream from the steamship wharves is full of anchored rafts with houses on them. No taxes. No difficulties with the police or shakedown from the politicians. Ample sanitation.

This floating city is more uptodate than the rustic port of Iquitos. There are warehouses with galvanized iron roofs, there are large grocerystores and hardwarestores, filling stations for motorboats and outboards. There is a goodsized clinic advertising the names of a number of doctors. There are repair-shops, warehouses of wholesale merchants who advertize for pelts and crocodile and snake skins, restaurants, cafés and bars, a barbershop.

Watermen, who skull small skiffs or row blue and green painted boats, take the place of taxicabs. They row standing, leaning forward on their oars. Canoes peddling hot coffee from raft to raft have romantic names like *Star of the Dawn.* A motorized coffee boat is labeled *Café Jango,* after the nick-name of the President of the Republic.

The floating city has a thriving air that is lacking in dry-land Manaus. Motor launches and small steamers crowded with passengers come and go. Canoes dart back and forth. Afloat you are free from the frustrating heat that acts like a leaden drag on every movement.

The Junction of the Waters

Invited for a fishing trip on an official cabin cruiser we rejoice in the coolness of the air over the moving water. The boat makes its own breeze. As he picks his way out through the skiffs and canoes towards the center of the river the man at the wheel points out people scooping up water in buckets. The dwellers on the *flutuantes* get their water from the middle of the river where it is reputed to be cleaner.

The waters of the Rio Negro really are black. The boat skims fast over the smooth lacquer surface. We are trolling with very large spoons on heavy nylon line. We are told that the river fish when they bite come big. This does not turn out to be the day.

There is a great deal to look at as we skirt the shore opposite the city. It is a day of blue sky and a thousand pale lavender-shadowed white blobs of cloud. The greens of the trees which stand kneedeep out of the dark water are incredibly varied. Palms of different shapes sprout out at all sorts of angles. There are misty thickets of bamboo and huge broadleaved arboreal monsters and spindly saplings with fine pale-green foliage. One of the characteristics of the Amazon forest is the fantastic number of different species to be found in any patch of woodland. You hardly see the same tree twice.

From reeds and floating islands and fallen logs, herons rise, kingfishers, ducks of all sorts. The colors of a butterfly will catch the sun as it flutters out from the forest shadows. A clearing, banana leaves swaying in the wind, tall papayas lifting their clusters of green fruit above the everpresent underbrush of manioc will announce a dwelling, sometimes a shack of boards with a roof of rough shingles, but more often a mere shelter of poles thatched with palm. Always there's a canoe. This is a population that lives by the river.

We leave the main stream of the river and plough through a network of narrow canals known as *igarapés*. Though there are differences in the style of boatbuilding and in the shape of their paddles, the people we pass are remarkably like the people we saw in riverside settlements a thousand miles upstream. There is a definite Amazonian type.

Here, if anything, the people seem poorer. Clothes are more ragged, children more naked, utensils more scanty. Sitting on top of the cabin as the boat chugs through the narrow watercourses is almost like visiting the people in their houses. Each house is open to inspection as the boat glides by. It is a life of total poverty; still the people have an independent air. Each house has its own canoes. The better off have outboards, fishnets hung to dry.

Longeared zebu cattle and waterbuffalo wade in distant drowned pastures. Through the more traveled igarapés steamboats ply, headed for distant settlements, towing behind them congeries of various craft. Cargoes are hidden from the sun by layers of large leaves.

In the pondlike head of one inlet, set around with big globular trees that give the effect of willows, we haul in our lines and ask a fisherman why we are not catching any fish.

High water, he answers immediately. The fish are feeding far inland in places where a boat like ours can never penetrate.

He is a tobaccocolored man with a wrinkled face and a long sharp nose jutting out from under the brim of his straw hat. He has a small neat canoe and a wellmade paddle. He paddles in the bow. Within easy reach he has a casting net, a couple of fishspears and a bow with long arrows. Beside them lie some coiled fishing lines and an antique shotgun. He controls his dugout canoe with hardly an effort of the arm.

Where is he going? "Fishing," he says, with a flash of his

eye, "or perhaps to hunt." He spins the canoe around and heads for a narrow watercourse much too small for our big lumbering motor cruiser. With the air of being monarch of all he surveys he disappears among the trees.

We double back through another narrow passage. We skirt rough wharves and settlements. We explore vast lakelike stretches of water bordering on the Rio Solimoes where gulls circle as over the ocean. Suddenly we are speeding out from a point of land into the junction of two streams. The man at the wheel follows a foamy path of spinning eddies that stretches like a seam between the rivers. On one side is the buffcolored flood of the Solimoes, on the other the dense black flood of the Rio Negro. For a long distance the two waters churn together without mixing. The cruiser staggers from the force of the eddies.

"See," cries the man at the wheel, "they don't want to mix . . ." As he brings the cruiser around in a wide circle he gives a sweep of his hand to point out the wilderness of wide waters which dwarfs the receding forested banks as they melt into the horizon, "but when they mix they form the Amazon."

VI

BRASÍLA REVISITED

"The Bestlaid Plans" . . .

You drive out to the airport in the steaming dark over the rackety cobbles of Manaus: you step into a jet plane and in four hours and a half you are in Brasília. It is the greatest contrast imaginable. Manaus is as redolent of the nineteenth century as a story by Jules Verne. The air is dense with green exhalations of the rainforest. Brasília is an arid red. The sun is hot but the air has a cool upland tang. The glimpses, as the plane banks for a landing, of glass and concrete constructions spread like an unfinished world's fair along the red ridge, between the two arms of the lake, are desperately contemporary. You are reminded of the story that's going the rounds about how a visiting Russian astronaut cried out on landing in Brasília: "I hadn't expected to reach Mars so soon."

In New York Brazilians told us: You mustn't go to the hotel that was new four years ago. You must go to the new hotel. We found the new new hotel, though of course many floors were still unfinished, to be remarkably pleasant, with its big kidneyshaped swimming pool in the sunny central court, which was flanked by a firstrate restaurant. Under the same management as the Jaraguá in São Paulo it is probably one of the best in South America.

The Nacional stands on a rise overlooking the central bus station where the arterial roads that form the city's backbone —the fuselage of Lucio Costa's jet plane—converge through cloverleaves into the roads that serve the wings. From the front door you look out across a rubbly hillside which will someday be Lucio Costa's modern Montmartre, past large Park Avenue type office buildings occupied by banks and insurance companies, down what corresponds to the mall in Washington, D.C. towards the shining tileshaped twin skyscrapers of the congressional offices. The confusing pile of masonry beyond the bus station will eventually become the white marble pyramid which will house Niemeyer's interlocking theaters.

To get from the hotel to the bus station on foot is a scramble. If paths for pedestrians were included in the plans, they haven't been built yet. There are of course no traffic lights. You have to wait for a lull and lope across the broad curving roadways as best you can. Many a pedestrian, so people tell us, has already lost his life on his way to the bus station.

When you finally reach the platform you can walk around in safety. Shining new Mercedes-Benz buses, produced in São Paulo, come in from all directions: Belo Horizonte, Anápolis, Ceres, Goiânia. Escalators take you to the upper levels. There are small stores, newsstands, snackbars, and coffee bars. The place has a cheerful practical look, except that the smooth-finished white concrete of the underpasses is already stained by the pervasive red dust.

There's no way to see the town without a car. In Brasília a man without a car is a secondclass citizen. The poorer inhabitants will have to grow wheels instead of feet.

The two buildings that flank the Congress Square, the Palacio do Planalto for the executive departments, and the Supreme Court building, are oblongs of transparent glass, each shaded by a broad slab of concrete supported by delicate white buttresscolumns. To my way of thinking they are among Niemeyer's best. Suited to the climate and the landscape. Fine examples of his paper cutout style. So are the odd little presidential chapel (which according to some irreverent people looks more like a urinal than a house of worship) and the charmingly simple Church of Our Lady of Fátima.

The congress building itself seems to me to be a conspicuous failure. The interior is cramped and illplanned for its purpose. There is a frivolous ugliness about the exterior hard to explain in a designer with such great talent for sculptural effects. Jefferson used to call architecture the most important of the arts "because it showed so much." Possibly the design of the congress hall expresses the faithful Communist's scorn for representative democracy.

Niemeyer's cathedral, an enormous coronet of stressed concrete, remains unfinished. The design calls for glass to fill in the spaces between the soaring piers. It is impressive as it is. One wonders whether it should ever be finished.

Though the long horizontals of the apartment buildings suit the city plan better than the occasional outbreak of New York style skyscrapers, the routine monotony of their design becomes depressing. The apartments themselves, seen from the inside, show little interest on the part of the designers for the needs of the people who have to live in them. The rows of identical concrete hutches for lower income renters express, even more perfectly than some federal housing in the United States, the twentieth century bureaucrat's disdain of the faceless multitudes to whose interests he is supposed to be devoted and whose exploitation furnishes his keep. The worst shack in the adjacent shantytowns of Cidade Livre or Taguatinga would be a better place to live.

Still, even after canvassing all the objections, you have to admit that the designers of Brasília have created a magnificent frame for a future city. The long straight thoroughfares, the vast open spaces between low white buildings are exhilarating. It's a city for the automotive age, for the age of jets and helicopters. Its vast spaces match the vast smooth arid ridges of the landscape of the planalto.

The lake greatly enhances the effect of the city and of the landscape. It is blue. I was afraid it would turn out muddy. It reflects the desert clouds and the gaudy sunsets and the bright firmament of the upland nights. There's a yachtclub and sailboats. We saw people fishing in it. Competent engineers after my last visit had told me so much about the possibility of seepage through the earth dam, that I had ceased to believe in the lake, but there it is, and protected from pollution by what looks to a layman like a thoroughly adequate sewage disposal plant.

Already signs are appearing of a post-Niemeyer architecture. The University of Brasília, which was only started some eight months back, is already conducting classes amid the hammering of carpenters and the dust of construction. Students on their way to lectures step over candongos laying tiled floors. The one building that's almost finished, named Os Dois Candongos for two bricklayers who were killed in its construction, offers a series of wellproportioned whitewalled halls, some lit from above and some from the side, which open on patios landscaped with specimens of the native vegetation of the planalto. It's all in human scale. A skillful balance—important under that glary sky—seems to have been struck between too little and too much light in the classrooms.

Courses in law, administration, humanities, Portuguese literature are already functioning. There is a school of architecture headed by Alcides da Rocha Miranda who designed the buildings we walked through. The curriculum so we were told is modeled on that of North American universities, and there is considerable emphasis, unusual in Brazil, on night school and extension courses for boys and girls who have to work to support themselves. The homey dormitory in frame and plaster with Japanese style woodwork balconies is a pleasure to look at after so much glass and concrete.

In the cafeteria there some of the teachers fed us one of the best *feijoadas* I ever ate. Feijoada is the Boston baked beans of Brazil and oddly enough also tends to appear on Saturdays. If the instruction proves as good as the cookery the University of Brasília should go far.

The Japanese, by the way, have added greatly to the variety of the architecture of Brasília by the daintily proportioned chancellery they have put up on their embassy lot. Our State Department, too, has done well with its chancellery. The courtyard is unusually attractive. There, and, in some of the suburban houses across the lake, you can see some intimation of the appearance of a Brasília style, suited to the light and to the climate and to the needs of the human beings who are going to inhabit the city.

When Oscar Niemeyer put up a residence to live in himself, way out of town near the country club, he built himself an oblong house with a tile roof and tall windows in the simple Brazilian colonial style which, in the first giddy enthusiasm for Le Corbusier's glass and steel, used to be considered hopelessly outmoded. People tell you he only built it to please his wife, but there it is.

How to Till the Planalto

Brasília is hungry for green. In areas laid out for parks and squares you see expanses of driedup turf, dead saplings, shriveled shrubberies testifying to the unsuccessful efforts of some municipal gardener. Not even palms seem to be doing well. Vegetation has a look of struggling not only against drought but against some peculiar quality in the soil.

Four years before we had seen the grim faces of a Japanese family trying, in what looked like a tolerable piece of bottomland, to grow truck crops. Even their hardiest vegetables, like cabbage and squash, had a sickly look. If the Japanese can't grow vegetables on a piece of land, there is something wrong.

After considerable asking around we were introduced to a gentleman from Paraná. He had emigrated to Brazil from Germany thirtyseven years before. He started as an interpreter with the federal Department of Agriculture, became a Brazilian citizen, and now owned land in Paraná where he did well, so he said, with the sale of timber. He also raised coffee and longstaple cotton. He was in Brasília to set up a tourist agency. With his help we found the agricultural experiment station at Sucupira.

The Brazilian agronomist in charge immediately cried out that he'd lost his Americans. The place had been set up under Point Four. He'd had a Texan, a Virginian, a Californian, and a man from Minnesota. He couldn't speak too highly of their work. He missed them as friends. When the Point Four money ran out they'd had to pack up and go home.

When the tug of war between the Brazilian congress and President Goulart was resolved so that the federal government got moving again, he hoped to secure Brazilian funds through the Ministry for Agriculture. Now everything was at a standstill. His tractors and mowers were all American. He needed parts. But the first thing he'd do, he said, was to get his American agronomists back. They had promised to come.

He drove us around the fields they had planted in various grasses on terraced hillsides. Some were local and some imported. Many of them looked flourishing. He said that by planting the proper grasses there were plenty of places in the outskirts of Brasília where you could graze cattle successfully. The soils of the planalto, he claimed, had the chemical nutrients needed for agriculture. Only they were locked up. In the States we could use lime to unlock our soils. Here the formula would have to be different but it was known. Technically the problem was solved. It was a question of funds.

Driving back we passed a cutting for the railroad. I said I'd been told the railroad line had been abandoned. It seemed a pity. Quite the contrary, said our friend from Paraná. There were only twelve more kilometers of track left to lay of a broad gauge line all the way from Belo Horizonte. Freight-service would start by the end of the year. Passengers would continue to use buses and planes.

When he deposited us back at the hotel he showed us what he had in his pockets. Cloth bags full of topazes and aqua-marine. He'd been to Cristalina, only a short trip off the main road to Belo Horizonte. Of course there was the cost of cutting them, but in Cristalina you could pick topazes up off the street. His eyes sparkled like the gems. That was Brazil.

"And He saw that it was good"

One of the pleasantest things about this last visit to Bra-sília was to be driven around by Dr. Israél. Four years before we had seen him at work managing Novacap. He'd been the city's first *prefeito*, but now after five years of intense ad-ministrative effort, he had been retired by the Goulart ad-ministration. Brasília had become his whole life. He couldn't move away. He lived in the residential suburb across the lake. He must have gotten special soil somewhere. His gar-den was flourishing. He showed us roses in bloom.

We drove through immense bare expanses of parts of the city that were not even planned yet and around the lake shore to the dam and down to the hydroelectric plant by the water-fall below it. Young Germans from Siemens were putting through the last tests on the two freshly installed generators. There was room for one more when it was needed. Light and power in three weeks, they promised Dr. Israél. He grinned his longtoothed grin and slapped them on the back.

"You see . . . They said we'd have no lake. They said we'd have no power."

He took us to see the frame building at the highest point

of the surrounding country where he and President Kubitschek had their quarters in the early days. The place was already a public park and picnic ground, presided over by a new bronze statue of the former president.

You could still see the outlines of the old fazenda which had been the only inhabited spot when the city planners first arrived. The great gushing spring of clear water was still there in the gully among the tall trees but now it was enclosed in a wire fence to keep the picnickers at the park from straying into the adjacent grounds. The country club had taken over the fazenda's magnificent grove of mangoes for its own private picnickings. Four years before we looked out from under the great dark trees on an incredibly vast prospect of bare hills occupied only by termites and rheas, the odd longlegged wolves and the striped cats of the region. Now the hills were scarred with roads. There were crosshatchings of suburban constructions. Scraps of the city's skyline jutted up into the horizon.

It was a nostalgic expedition. Dr. Israél showed us the entrance to the beautiful house beside a small waterfall tumbling into a natural rock basin which he'd occupied as prefeito. The new prefeito lived there now. In the old days the place had been known by Dr. Israél's initials: I.P. The new administration made out that it was named after a yellowflowered tree that grows along the watercourses, called in those parts the *ipé*.

One of the inconveniences of life in Brasília in the summer of 1962 was that the light and power almost inevitably would fail just about seven every evening. Some said it was because the officials of the state of Goiás who controlled the hightension lines from the Cachoeira Dourada (the Golden Waterfall) on the Paranaíba River, from which the power came, would pull the switch as a hint that the federal city better hurry up and pay its bills. Even at the efficient Hotel Nacional, guests would be trapped in the elevators and imprisoned for hours. The forewarned would avoid the elevators at this time of day and grope their way with candles down the unfinished stairways to the lobby.

The lights failed the very night Dr. Israél invited us to dinner. As it was a moonless night we had to find his house by the light of the Milky Way. He gave one of his snorting laughs as he met us with a candle. "You saw the new generators," he said. "Come back a month from now and this won't happen."

VII

THE MOST DANGEROUS MAN

Campaign in the Grassroots

The first thing I saw when I stepped out of the hotel our first morning in Manaus was a curlyheaded young man in a doublebreasted caramelcolored suit. He was waving his arms and shouting in the middle of a crowd of market people and longshoremen. He was jumping up and down from sheer earnestness as he talked. He had a loudspeaker attached to his chest which seemed to be operated by a battery in the suitcase that lay at his feet. At first I thought he was selling patent medicine. It turned out he was a political candidate. Though it was early morning, the sun was hot. He'd already sweated through his doublebreasted suit. He was hoarse. His face was red. He was shouting so I couldn't follow what he was saying except that his platform was to drive thieves and robbers out of the legislature of the state of Amazonas. I remember thinking: if he's so hoarse and sweaty this early in the morning how is he going to last six weeks to election day?

The campaign of 1962, though only part of the federal congress, the state legislatures, and some governors were up for election, was one of the most hectic in Brazilian history. It looked as if politics had finally forged ahead of soccer. In Rio we found that something like seven hundred candidates were contesting fiftyseven seats, to be distributed according to proportional representation among thirteen parties, in the legislature of the new state of Guanabara. When the capital was moved to Brasília, the old federal district which comprised the area of the city of Rio de Janeiro became what the Cariocas like to call "the citystate" of Guanabara. The streets were so festooned with election posters you could hardly see the trees. A loudspeaker truck bellowed from every corner.

There were so many candidates they had been assigned numbers, like social security numbers.

A young man named Pedro Livio MacGregor—he got the name from a Scottish grandfather—who was a candidate for the Guanabara legislature, explained the electoral system to me. We were sitting at a table at the edge of the sunlight beside the wide swimmingpool in the courtyard of the Copacabana Palace Hotel. This is one of the spots in Rio where everybody meets everybody. Besides being a politician my informant was a Spiritualist minister.

The Brazilian *Spiritas* believe that they are in continuous communication with the dead; Jesus Christ in person continues to teach them from the other world. At their house of worship young MacGregor conducted a sort of settlement house for the favela dwellers, which included a clinic where doctors were available without charge. They distributed drugs and babyfoods free, along with advice as to how people should live their lives. "When they come, they know nothing," he said, "they are like animals, we have to teach them to clean their teeth and to wash their faces."

His enthusiasm for social service had induced him to run for office. As a Social Democrat (PSD), he relied heavily on the support of ex-President Kubitschek in his campaign.

Describing the elective system he emphasized the fact that really free elections were a novelty in Brazil. According to him the first was in 1955. Before that, particularly in the back country, people just took the ballots printed beforehand by the parties and handed out to them by the *coroneles* (the colonels), as the local bosses were called; and dropped them in the box. In 1955 official ballots were printed, as in the United States, on which the voter could mark his preference. This election of 1962 would be the first in which the printed ballot, with complete lists of candidates, would be practically nationwide. Another innovation would be that up to a certain date all parties would have free time in TV and radio.

"Everybody has agreed that this must be an honest election," he said with fervor. He was a rather pale man with extremely lucid eyes. His eyes glowed with enthusiasm. "In spite of everything democracy advances."

Award Winning Journalist

There is great fluidity about Brazilian politics as about everything else in that rapidly evolving country. Ever since the end of the Vargas regime the state governors have been increasing in importance. The first governor of Guanabara was Carlos Lacerda. His term still had two years to run. Although he himself was not a candidate for office, the fact that he is Brazil's most accomplished anti-Communist made him the chief voice of the opposition against the candidacy for the federal chamber of deputies of a gentleman named Leonel Brizola who was about to retire as governor of the *gaúcho* state of Rio Grande do Sul.

In Brazil, as in England, you don't have to be a resident of your constituency to run for offices in the national government. Although there were many local issues and local personalities involved, the underlying national issue of the campaign of 1962 was whether Brazil, in the so-called cold war, should incline towards Fidel Castro's Cuba and the Communist powers, or towards the United States, and its Alliance for Progress program. Lacerda opposed the Communists. Brizola spoke their language. In our curious age, when, among the Western peoples whose institutions the Communists are undermining, anyone who vigorously opposes them is spoken of as a controversial figure, Lacerda has been, almost since boyhood, the most controversial of controversial figures in Brazilian public life.

It was in Washington that I first met Carlos Lacerda.

Ever since our uproarious motor trip into the hills of Minas Gerais in the days when driving a car in backcountry Brazil was a sporting proposition I've always had my face fixed for a laugh when I went to call on the Whites. By the fall of 1952 they had moved to Washington from Rio. This time I could hear Bill's and Connie's voices laughing inside when I rang the doorbell of their Georgetown apartment.

From the livingroom I could hear a voice with a foreign accent pronouncing the words: "Oopaylong Ca-seedy." Immediately I was introduced to a tall strikingly handsome man. In one hand he was brandishing a pearlhandled cap pistol. A glittering holster was draped over one shoulder. Perched on his head above his shellrimmed glasses was a small boy's cowboy hat.

The Whites explained him as a Brazilian journalist who had come to Washington to receive an award from the Inter-American Press Association. His English was fluent but erratic. His high spirits were catching. He shared our taste for the absurd. We all laughed our heads off about Oopalong Ca-seedy.

Connie had been helping him buy Wild West equipment for his children before starting home. They had been showing it off to Bill with appropriate gestures. The Whites' living room was littered with wrapping paper, striped jumpers, cowboy suits, towheaded dolls, assorted gadgets from the Five and Ten.

His taxi was waiting to take him to the airport. We helped him pack up his purchases into a couple of shoppingbags and very reluctantly bade him goodby.

In the excitement I'd failed to catch his name. "He's the nicest man in Brazil," the Whites told me after he'd gone. "His name is Carlos Lacerda."

A number of years went by before I ran into Carlos Lacerda again at a luncheon in one of the mountain resorts near Petrópolis. The Brazilian friend who was driving us up from Rio started to tell his life history as soon as we were free of the dense traffic of the city.

In those days the Petrópolis road climbed the steep slope hairpin by hairpin through great trees and flowery underbrush. My friend would catch his breath in the middle of a sentence while he swung the little car around another curve. His wife could talk of nothing but how excited she was about meeting Carlos Lacerda. She'd voted for him twice, she said she was going to vote for him again. We were going to pick him up at his country place and take him along to lunch with a lady named Lota de Macedo Soares.

Dona Lota had just built the modernest of modern Brazilian houses. We were looking forward to seeing the house. Our friend's wife said she had seen plenty of modern houses. It was Lacerda she wanted to see.

"He's charming to meet," the husband said, "but when you put a typewriter in front of him he becomes vindictive. He's a terrible man. Didn't he kill Vargas?"

"I thought Vargas shot himself."

"Lacerda's attacks in his newspaper drove him to it . . . Carlos Lacerda's the most dangerous man in Brazil."

"How come?"

My Brazilian friend couldn't answer. He was busy avoiding an onrushing truck on a particularly sharp curve. We all breathed again when he pulled off the road at the top of the

hill to a stall where he bought us coffee and crisp little meat-
pies. While we munched, and looked down over the tops of
the trees at the incredible view of the bay of Guanabara sim-
mering in the sunny haze between purple toothshaped mountains, he continued his briefing.

Weaned on Controversy

Lacerda's ideas, began my friend, are those of many
generous-minded men in our time in many different countries the world over, but he takes them so seriously. He began
to laugh. The trouble with Carlos is that once he starts talking he doesn't know when to stop. Controversial. He can't
open his mouth without stirring up controversy.

He was brought up from the cradle in an atmosphere of
controversy. The whole family was in politics. Carlos was
born in Rio the year the First World War began, but his
grandfather, Sebastião Lacerda, who was a justice of the Brazilian Supreme Court, insisted on registering his birth at the
old family home at Vassouras on the Paraíba River in the
state of Rio de Janeiro.

The state of Rio, a weirdly beautiful region of halfaban-
doned great houses and plantations that have been running
down ever since the emancipation of the slaves, has always
been separate from the city, which in the days before the
federal district was moved into the interior, was the capital
of Brazil.

Carlos' father, Maurício Lacerda, was a rather erratic Socialist deputy. He came back from Europe after the Russian
revolution declaring himself to be a Maximalist. The Maxi-
malists were the extreme left wing of the Russian Socialists
before Lenin taught everybody in Russia to think the same
way. The father was too busy with a number of things to pay
much attention to his family, so young Carlos was raised at
his grandfather's place on the Paraíba River. This was a small
fruit farm established by Carlos' greatgrandparents. The wife,

who was Portuguese, sold mangoes while the husband, by profession a baker, baked bread. Out of the proceeds they sent Carlos' grandfather to study law in São Paulo where another member of the family had already made a name for himself as a jurist. Perhaps Carlos' countryman's fondness for growing things originated in these early days at Vassoura. He says the Paraíba River was as important to his boyhood as the Mississippi was to Mark Twain's.

Carlos was a precocious lad. At sixteen he was already on his own in Rio, studying law and picking up a little money writing for the newspapers. He was developing a prodigious ability for hard work.

This was in 1930, the year when a widespread rising of military men and politicians installed Getúlio Vargas in the presidency. Brazil was suffering its share of the political upheavals that followed in the wake of the Great Depression.

Vargas ousted the business-oriented regime of President Washington Luíz, who was such a good friend of the White House that Herbert Hoover sent him home on a battleship after a state visit to the United States. Washington Luíz was the last of a line of Brazilian statesmen who considered friendship with the United States virtually part of their oath of office. Now the stockmarket crash had made a dent in American prestige.

Portugal, Spain, and Italy were already under various sorts of Fascist dictatorships. Hitler's baleful star was rising in the north. Among the people of Europe Fascism was the rage. Vargas looked to Europe for guidance rather than to the United States.

Up to Vargas' time politics in Brazil had been the business of oligarchical groups. Vargas appealed to the masses. His eventual denial of any of the rights of political agitation helped by a spirit of contradiction to arouse the public and make politics one of the great Brazilian preoccupations.

Carlos Lacerda took to politics like a duck to water. He early showed a sharp pen for invective and a talent for public speaking. He had charm, good looks, and reckless personal courage. He was fired by all the enthusiasms of his father's utopian socialism.

Vargas' first administration started out in a New Dealish kind of way, aiming towards universal suffrage, including votes for women, the encouragement of labor unions to protect working people, the colonization of the west, the elimination of poverty and epidemic disease, a beginning of the social reforms progressive Brazilians had been demanding for years. Vargas had plans for Brazil that won the support of the young idealists.

Vargas had been Washington Luíz's Minister of the Treasury (Fazenda), but his political rearing was in the school of Borges de Madeiros, the ironfisted boss of his home state of Rio Grande do Sul on the turbulent southern border. This was gaúcho country where politicians still talked with the gun. Not that Vargas was a man of violence. Far from it. A small stoutish fellow with a benevolent smile and friendly wrinkles round his eyes, he was a conniving man who preferred to triumph by corrupting his enemies rather than by a direct show of force.

As Vargas watched the success overseas of Hitler's National Socialism and of Mussolini's Corporate State he began to plan something similar for Brazil. He began to appreciate the demagogic possibilities of an appeal to the masses. Through government subsidies and by planting his own men in their management he geared labor unions and student organizations, and much of big business, into his own political machine.

His twenty year rule determined the shape of Brazilian society for years to come. As the only politician who had ever paid attention to them he had the devotion of the urban working class. The coffee barons and the new industrial magnates of São Paulo trusted him to keep the working class in order. It was under Vargas that the strange link was formed between Brazilian big business and the Brazilian left. He dominated the Army and Navy through appointments and promotions, the press through his censorship bureau. Where he couldn't intimidate people he bought them.

His appetite for power grew with the exercise, until in 1937 he was ready to proclaim his *Estado Nôvo* (the New State). Patriarchal government has deep roots in Brazil. In colonial days the father had power of life and death. Plumpfaced subtly smiling innocent appearing Getúlio Vargas was presented as a benevolent father to the poor. This was Fascism Brazilian style.

Every career was closed to a nonconformist. The newspapers were forbidden to mention the word democracy.

For a while the Communists offered the only vocal opposition. It is easy to see how a fiery young law student with a passion for civil liberties should be attracted to them. In those days all oppression seemed to come from the Fascists. The Communists operated under the banner of the popular front. In Brazil particularly the Party had taken over a certain romantic aura with the conversion to Marxism of Luís Carlos Prestes. Captain Prestes was a romantic young officer of engineers who, after the failure of one of the many popular outbursts against the oligarchical regime of the twenties, led a column of revolting troops and assorted revolutionists through thousands of miles of the wilderness of Mato Grosso and kept them together for many months before he was forced to seek asylum in Bolívia. The adventures of the Prestes column turned all the young men's heads. Lacerda now says it was only the tactics of the popular front that kept him from formally becoming a party member.

As student leader of a protest organization called the Alianza Libertadora he traveled about the country addressing meetings in behalf of laborleaders and anti-Fascists. When

there was a strike he was for the strikers. His heated protests
appeared in clandestine publications. Whenever Vargas' police
scented trouble Carlos Lacerda was among those they carried
off to the jug. When he wasn't in jail he was in hiding.

He married at twentythree. When his first child was on the
way he had to come to grips with the problem of making a
living. Friends talked Vargas into letting the young firebrand
out from one of his many jailings on the understanding that
he would forego politics.

He went to work for a nonpartisan journal of economics.
He did spreads for an advertising agency. He won fame as re-
porter for *O Jornal*, the key newspaper of the *Diários Associados*, Chateaubriand's national chain, which was the Brazilian counterpart of the Hearst or Scripps-Howard chains in the
United States. In 1943 he was made city editor.

How Vargas Became a Good Neighbor

After the American entrance into the war against Hitler,
and particularly when the military fortunes of the Axis powers began to dim, a change came over the Estado Nôvo. Fascist was becoming a term of abuse. Vargas began to model
his image more on Franklin D. Roosevelt and less on Mussolini. The good neighbor began to win over the screaming
dictator.

Lacerda by this time was the outstanding journalist in Rio.
He did everything he could to help the process on. He
scooped the nation on the Normandy landings.

It was Carlos Lacerda who accomplished the first break
through Vargas' press censorship. José Américo, a revered political oldtimer who had supported Vargas in his reforming
days, gave Lacerda an interview in which he demanded free
elections and a free press. *O Jornal* wouldn't print it. For
twenty days Lacerda tramped about Rio looking for an editor
with nerve enough to print Américo's statement.

When the *Correo da Manhã* took the risk the result was sensational. The logjam broke. Protests against dictatorship erupted all over the country. The *Correo da Manhã* featured Lacerda's columns from then on.

By breaking with the Diários Associados, Lacerda, without a second thought, gave up an assured career as one of Brazil's best paid journalists. During the same period he became estranged from the Communists. When Lacerda called for civil liberties and a government of law, he meant what he said. Stalin's purges and the Hitler-Stalin pact convinced him that nothing was to be hoped from the Communists towards the sort of reforms he wanted. When the Brazilian Communists, after Moscow's scrapping of the tactics of the popular front, took to supporting the Vargas dictatorship, Lacerda's disillusionment was complete.

The incident he says revolted him most was the appearance of Luís Carlos Prestes, by this time a docile party puppet, on the same platform with Getúlio Vargas. Vargas not only had nabbed Prestes and kept him in jail for years when he ventured home from exile, but at the height of his pro-Nazi enthusiasm he had turned Prestes' German-Jewish wife over to the German authorities to be done to death in one of Hitler's concentration camps.

It took the threat of a military coup to induce Vargas to allow presidential elections in 1945. Lacerda jumped back into politics with both feet.

He now hated Vargas and the Communists with equal fervor. The candidate for the presidency whom José Américo brought forward as spokesman for the hastily improvised antitotalitarian coalition, which took the name of the *União Democrático Nacional*, was one of the few army officers of rank who could not be accused of collaboration with the dictatorship, Brigadier Eduardo Gomes. Gomes was highly esteemed in democratic circles in the army, navy and aircorps

as the sole survivor of the forlorn uprising of the Fort of Copacabana in the early twenties. Lacerda threw everything he
had into campaigning for Gomes.

In the course of the campaign he vented his bitterness
against the Communists by daily taking the hide off a gentleman named Iedo Fuiza whom they were running for the presidency. Lacerda claimed that Fuiza had made a fortune in real
estate while he headed the National Department of Railroads,
and could not possibly believe in the Communist aims; he
ended every speech by calling him a hypocritical rat.

The response of the Communists was to turn Lacerda in to
the police as a Trotzkyite. For one last time he found himself in Vargas' hoosegow.

That genial despot, though at one time he hadn't allowed
Franklin D. Roosevelt's speeches to be printed in the Brazilian newspapers, was proving the sincerity of his conversion to
the cause of democracy by encouraging the Americans to build
and operate airfields on the eastern bulge for the airlift
to Africa. He further conciliated pro-Allied opinion at home
and abroad by letting the Brazilian Army send an expedition-
ary force to Italy which gave a good account of itself fighting
alongside the Americans.

The wily old dictator was executing a skillful retreat from
the Estado Nôvo. The Brazilians wanted political parties?
Well they should have them. He set up a labor party, the
Partido Trabalhista Brasileiro, based on his own subsidized
labor unions. He did grudgingly allow free unions but they
had to pay their own bills. To make sure the Labor Party
should carry out his wishes, he put his own son in as chairman.

Opposition? Very good, but it must be loyal. To keep the
opposition in the family Vargas saw to it that his daughter's
husband should preside over the competing *Partido Social
Democrático.* Having assured his machine of control of a majority of the votes he felt it safe to allow the orators of the
Democratic Union to talk as much as they wanted to.

The Tribune of the Press

Carlos Lacerda became the Patrick Henry of the Democratic Union. He discovered that his voice was effective over the radio. All Rio listened to his broadcasts lambasting the corruptions of the Vargas regime and its Communist supporters. The argument became highly personal when a Communist gang waylaid him one night on his way home from the radio station and beat him up severely. His answer was to take a course in judo for selfdefense and to redouble the sarcasm of his attacks. At the same time he conducted a vigorously controversial column in the *Correio da Manhã* which he called *Tribuna da Imprensa* (the Tribune of the Press).

Vargas' Minister of War, General Eurico Gaspar Dutra, was elected President for a fiveyear term by a large majority in 1945. The Vargas machine conducted the election. The electoral boards ruled that approved members of Vargas' labor unions should be registered automatically. They could be trusted to vote as they were told. Other people had to establish their right to vote by a literacy test.

Though Dutra was elected by the Vargas machine, he was a somewhat independent minded man and could rely on the support of a large body of pro-Allied opinion which had become increasingly vocal with the decay of the censorship. Brazilian historians speak of Dutra's presidency as a period of democratic convalescence.

Parties were allowed to develop independently. Released from the threat of intervention by the federal government, political organizing began to center in the states. In São Paulo and Minas Gerais local machines flourished.

In Rio Carlos Lacerda was in 1946 elected to his first public office as *vereador* (city counselor) by a large majority. The very violence of his enemies helped bring him support. Three years later he gave the name of his column "Tribuna da Imprensa" to a newspaper of his own. It was the first newspaper in Brazil established by public subscription. People from all walks of life bought stock. Several wellknown soccer players chipped in. One day a group of cleaning women turned up at Lacerda's office offering to contribute a few crumpled ten-cruzeiro bills.

President Dutra's term would end in 1951. According to the current wording of the so often rewritten Brazilian constitution he could not succeed himself. Vargas, who had spent the five years in rural retirement on his estate at São Borja on the Argentine border, was urged to try again.

He had been watching his apt pupil, Juan Perón, apply his own version of the Estado Nôvo to the distracted republic on the River Plate. President Roosevelt's death and the breakdown of leadership from Washington had left a political vacuum in the world. Communism poured in. The stock of democracy was sinking again on the international market.

Getúlio's Return

Vargas was old and tired but his henchmen were hungry. The old machine was still intact in the Labor Party and the labor unions. He had an active yellow press at his disposal. His supporters united the Communists, whose watchword was now down with everything connected with the United States, with the leftovers of Fascist nationalism, the frustrated radicals who still dreamed of a socialist utopia, and with local industrialists who feared foreign competition. An adept in the corruptions of politics Vargas played on these factions with a master hand and easily defeated the colorless candidate of the Social Democrats and the Democratic Union's virtuous brigadier.

The Brazilians were a youthful people, was how Lacerda explained the defeat of his party, statistically more than half the population was under eighteen. Many of the voters in 1951 were too young to remember the oppressions of the Estado

Nôvo. Lacerda himself was bitterly reproached for libeling a good old man.

The old dictator's victory threw the moderate politicians into confusion. People braced themselves for a new bout of dictatorship. The Democratic Union almost fell apart. Lacerda's *Tribune of the Press*, with much greater influence than could be accounted for by its circulation, remained as a rallying ground for those opposed to totalitarian schemes.

After five quiet years, busied only with his ranches and his family, the good old man from São Borja moved back into the presidential palace in Rio. The ex-dictator felt a fatherly gratitude towards his people for having re-elected him their constitutional President. He sincerely believed he knew what was best for the Brazilians, but the Brazil he returned to was a changed country.

American financing during the war had given Brazilian manufacturing just the push forward it needed. Volta Redonda was already turning out steel. Fortunes were being made producing consumer goods in São Paulo in spite of the collapse of the world market in coffee. Industries were spreading out from Rio and São Paulo into the hinterlands of Minas Gerais. Roads were beginning to improve. Public health measures stimulated the growth of population. The cities were bursting at the seams. Contractors were getting rich building apartments. In spite of an adverse balance of payments, inflation, bluesky speculation and every fiscal ill on the calendar, Brazil was on the verge of an industrial boom.

President Vargas, now a satisfied aging man with the old benevolent smile on his face, only wanted an easy life. He wanted everybody to think well of him without worrying too much about overcrowded cities or the problems of financing a vast irregularly developing nation.

The trouble was that his supporters, the party stalwarts who had dragooned the workingclass voters into electing him, weren't satisfied. They were hungry. They couldn't wait to fill their pockets. Even the members of Vargas' own family became infected by the get rich quick fever. The lobbies of the presidential palace swarmed with influence peddlers and fixers, many of them gangsters and lowlives with police records. In the memory of man no one had seen such barefaced thievery as went on in Vargas' last administration.

The Voice of Opposition

As scandal after scandal boiled to the surface, Carlos Lacerda made it his business to see that nobody forgot them. He was determined to stave off a dictatorship. After a second term as city counselor he was planning to run for the federal Chamber of Deputies.

He had discovered television. His face on the screen became a trade mark. The firm jaw, the clearcut nose between the dark shell rims of his glasses, through which glowing dark eyes burned into the consciousness of the audience, were unforgettable. Without talking down to the crowd he developed a way of explaining complicated problems so that they became understandable to a great many different sorts of people. Spoken, his editorials were even more effective than in the printed column.

As Vargas' presidential term drew to a close the old man began to see retirement staring him in the face. Though a presidential campaign was already underweigh, designing voices whispered in the President's ear that maybe all these elections weren't in the national interest after all. The Vargas politicians wanted to hold onto their jobs. Rio hummed with rumors of a new dictatorship.

In his column in his afternoon paper Lacerda analyzed each new revelation. Evenings on TV he brought in facts and figures to back up his assertions. He drew charts of government malfeasance on a blackboard. His voice stung like a whip. It

began to be reported that the men of Vargas' personal bodyguard were threatening to kill him if he didn't cease from his
attacks. Lacerda shared his scorn of these threats with his TV
audience.

Among the military there was considerable sympathy for
Lacerda's campaign. His support of Brigadier Gomes had
made him popular among the younger officers. They couldn't
help admiring his courage. They shared his dismay at the corruption of the Vargas administration. Supporters in the Air
Force took turns accompanying him home at night. They
wanted to be sure he had a witness in case there was an at-
tempt on his life. None of them imagined anybody would be
so reckless as to shoot at an army officer.

The manifesto of a group of colonels had forced the resignation of one of Vargas' ministers. The Ministry of Labor
was politically the keystone of his administration because it
controlled the patronage of the labor unions. Vargas' Minister
of Labor was a young neighbor from São Borja whom the old
man had taken a fancy to and whose debut in politics he had
sponsored in his home state. João Goulart was an attractive
young landowner of great wealth reputed to be a crony of
Perón's. The colonels accused him of planning a syndicalist
republic, *peronista* style. Reluctantly Vargas submitted to the
retirement of Minister Goulart.

Not long after, Lacerda was slated to address a political
meeting. That night it was the turn of Major Rubens Vaz
to see that he got home safely. Lacerda lived at that time in
Copacabana, the famous beach resort which the first building
boom of the thirties had made part of the city of Rio, in a
new apartment house on a treelined street overshadowed by
the mountain and the tall buildings. Broadleaved trees over-
growing the streetlamps made the sidewalks dark. The litter
of construction was everywhere. As Lacerda and Major Vaz
climbed out of their car at Lacerda's front door somebody

started shooting at them from across the street. Lacerda returned the fire. Major Vaz, who was unarmed, was killed. Lacerda was shot in the foot. The assailants escaped.

The Crime on Toneleros Street

When Vargas' police appeared on the scene they tried to make it appear that it was Lacerda, while firing at an imaginary gunman, who had killed Major Vaz.

Major Vaz had a wife and children. He was a popular young officer. His murder infuriated his comrades in the Air Force. Brushing the police aside, a group of senior officers decided to hold their own inquest. It became clear that the murder was instigated by a Negro named Fortunato Gregório who was known as the "black angel" of Vargas' personal bodyguard. He eventually confessed to having hired the gunman to do the job and was sent to jail for twenty years, there being no death penalty in Brazil.

The press, the houses of Congress, the military clubs rang with denunciations of the crime on Toneleros Street. Demands for President Vargas' resignation were heard on every hand. The old man was terribly shaken by Gregório's confession and by definite proof which was placed on his desk that his own children were trading on his name in all sorts of financial deals. At a meeting of his Cabinet the night of August 23 he spoke despairingly of "the sea of mud" under the presidential palace and consented, after much urging, if not to resign, at least to retire from the government.

After the cabinet meeting President Vargas went to his room in the early hours of August 24 and there shot himself through the heart.

"The odd thing about it," said my friend when he broke off the story, "is that Vargas' suicide made him a national hero . . . the Brazilians are a sentimental people."

"But how can they blame Lacerda for it?" cried his wife impatiently. "It was Lacerda who was the hero."

Sunday Lunch in Petrópolis

We had driven out beyond the cobbled treeshaded avenues of Petrópolis into a broad rimrocked valley. Brilliantly green vegetation sprouting with all kinds of flowers overflowed the stone garden walls on either side of the road.

When we reached Lacerda's country place my friend parked his little car in an embrasure in one of the walls and led the way up some stone steps through a tunnel of bougainvillaea into a flagged patio. Everything was so full of flowering plants you couldn't tell which was the garden and which was the house.

Lacerda set down a flowerpot as he came out to greet us. He was tanned, very much the sunburned Apollo in shell-rimmed spectacles. He was completely preoccupied with his gardening operations. As we walked about his orchard and vegetable garden he introduced each plant and tree as if it were a person.

He had reason to be proud of his plantings. The valleys in the mountains around Petrópolis are one of those marvelous regions where plants from the tropical and temperate zones flourish with equal profusion. There are orchids along with nasturtiums. Cabbages grow next to pineapples. Beside mangoes grow guavas, oranges, and apricots, and even occasionally an apple tree. Lacerda was particularly proud of his apple tree.

Somebody said the place was like the Garden of Eden. "Naturally. We are in my native state of Rio de Janeiro," Lacerda answered dreamily in English. "It is truly a paradise"—he laughed—"where only man is vile . . . Maybe not so vile. Let's give him a chance."

We met his wife, who looked much too young to be the mother of two wellgrown boys and a girl. Lacerda himself looked younger than I had remembered. There was an air of

youthfulness and closeknit intimacy about the whole family.
You felt they were all in it together.

Dona Lota's house, built by Sérgio Bernardes of glass and
steel beside a cascading brook, was something to see, though
one skeptic did mutter into another skeptic's ear that it did
look a little like the model of an oldfashioned railroad station.
There was a pleasant gathering at lunch: the architect Bernardes, an eminent historian, a number of people interested
primarily in painting and sculpture. The talk, half in English,
half in Portuguese, was about Picasso and Léger and books
and St. John Perse and the new museum for modern art which
was going up in Rio. Lacerda was at home in all this. He
showed a flair for painting. He expressed the reasoned likes
and dislikes of a man who did his own reading and used his
own eyes and his own ears. His remarks had a humorous tone
that kept us all laughing. Not a word about contemporary politics.

On the way back down the mountain my friend's wife said
she was a little let down. It was as if we had been lunching in
Paris, instead of Brazil. She had expected Lacerda to be more
forceful. "It's a Sunday," said her husband soothingly, "a man
can't be forceful every day of the week."

The Cruise of the Tamandaré

A few nights later at the apartment on Toneleros Street,
where he still lived, Lacerda himself described the scramble
of events so unfortunate for his Democratic Union that followed Vargas' death. He didn't spare himself. He gave a comi-
cal cast to the recital of his political misadventures.

After Vargas' death Vice-President Café Filho, a wellmean-
ing gentleman from one of the small northeastern states, took
over the presidency in due form. He had been on good terms
with the old man and took the attitude that as interim President his only business was to see that the elections were peace-
fully conducted.

The country was preoccupied with the funeral eulogies of
the great Getúlio. The industrial workers felt that they had
lost their best friend. Even among the growing middle class,
who tended to sympathize with the Democratic Union, it was
admitted that Vargas had broadened the base of participation
in political life. Every Brazilian now felt himself a citizen. The
crimes and corruptions of the dictatorship were forgotten in
the general mourning.

Lacerda, in speeches and editorials, was driving for a com-
plete cleanup of the remnants of the Vargas regime. In his
Tribune of the Press he called for an end of machine politics.
He was piling up votes for his candidacy for the Chamber of
Deputies.

Party labels have little meaning in Brazil. With the relaxa-
tion of Vargas' heavy centralizing hand the national parties
fell under the command of local leaders in the different states.
The state governors became powerful figures. Groupings of local politicians resulted in splinterings and coalitions. Dozens
of minor parties came into being. In São Paulo, for example,
a pokerfaced politico named Adhemar de Barros used his patronage as governor to build up a Social Progressive Party of
his own. In Minas Gerais the governor, Dr. Juscelino Kubitschek, was being groomed for the presidency by his local Social Democratic machine. From their stronghold in Rio
Grande do Sul, under the banner of a testament supposedly
written out by Vargas before his death, João Goulart and his
brotherinlaw Leonel Brizola kept Vargas' Labor Party intact,
though its greatest strength still lay in the labor unions of the
city of Rio.

In the 1955 election, through a deal with the Labor Party
which resulted in João Goulart's being chosen Vice-President,
Kubitschek carried the presidency. The Communists claimed
that it was their backing that clinched his election.

Reform was in the air all the same. A brash young man
whose emblem was a new broom and whose motto was

a clean sweep had defeated Adhemar de Barros in São Paulo the year before. Honesty in office and efficient administration were Jânio Quadros' warcries. His first act was to have his predecessor indicted for peculation. The same reform movement carried Carlos Lacerda to the Chamber of Deputies by a very large vote.

The Democratic Union, to which Lacerda belonged, questioned Kubitschek's election as having been put through with the support of the illegal Communist party and by the discredited methods of the Vargas machine. There was a head-on confrontation of forces.

In such moments in Brazil the armed services tend to be the decisive factor. A large part of the Army went along with Café Filho's Minister of War, General Teixeira Lott, in endorsing Kubitschek's election. On the other hand there were groups of officers, particularly in the Navy and Air Force, who wanted a general housecleaning under the auspices of Brigadier Gomes. All Rio whispered of a *coup d'état*. The tension reached such a point that President Café Filho collapsed from a heart attack and was placed by his doctors in an oxygen tent in a hospital, incommunicado.

Congress forthwith declared the presidency vacant and installed Carlos Luz, the Speaker of the House, as constitutional President. Carlos Luz was a Social Democrat with reformist sympathies. It seemed the Godgiven moment for the reformers to take power. Luz demanded General Lott's resignation and appointed another general in his place as Minister of War.

General Lott resigned all right, but immediately he sent troops he could trust to occupy key points in Rio. A coup to forestall a coup, he called it. Labor and some Social Democrat factions in the congress declared Luz deposed, and appointed their adherent, Nereu Ramos, who, as presiding officer of the Senate, was next in order of succession, President in his stead.

For a few hours it looked like civil war. Café Filho lay

helpless in his oxygen tent. Brigadier Gomes, still the hope of the Democratic Union, started for São Paulo where he hoped to recruit adherents. Claiming he was still constitutional President, Carlos Luz gathered his supporters about him and they all trouped aboard an old American cruiser renamed the *Tamandaré*. The commander, a sympathizer, received him with full honors. Carlos Lacerda, still only deputy elect, went along.

The cruise of the *Tamandaré* proved a fizzle. Orders were issued to proceed at full steam to Santos, where the harbor forts were in the hands of officers favorable to Carlos Luz, but there was very little coal in the bunkers and part of the crew was on shore leave. During the hours that went by before the cruiser could put to sea General Lott had Gomes intercepted and sent emissaries to win over the garrisons of São Paulo and Santos.

Lott's orders were for the *Tamandaré* to stay in port. When the cruiser, with barely enough steam for half speed, did manage to weigh anchor and to head out across the bar for the open sea, the Ministry of War sent word to the forts to stop her, by gunfire if necessary. When the shells came shrieking across the water the group on the bridge of the *Tamandaré* decided not to return the fire. They were afraid of missing the forts and hitting the civilian buildings behind. Most of them had families in Copacabana. Several shells came perilously close until a freighter got between the cruiser and the forts. The skipper didn't seem to notice that a battle was in progress. That caused the forts to cease firing, for fear of hitting the freighter.

The cruiser continued down the coast until the radio announced that the Santos forts had gone over to General Lott. Then the *Tamandaré* ignominiously turned tail and steamed back to her berth in the navy yard.

The deposed President and his entourage were branded as mutineers by the new government. They scattered through the city to seek political asylum. Carlos Lacerda took refuge in the Cuban embassy. He'll tell you laughingly that politically speaking this was the lowest moment of his life. A few days later he was allowed to leave with his family for the United States in voluntary exile.

Nereu Ramos turned over the presidency to Juscelino Kubitschek in due course.

The Lacerda family remained in the United States for several months. The boys went to school in Norwalk, Connecticut, and Carlos worked as a translator for subtitles for motion pictures, and as foreign correspondent for the *Estado de São Paulo*. He set himself with his usual feverish energy to improve his knowledge of English. Money ran low so the Lacerdas went to Lisbon, where living was cheaper than in Norwalk. When Carlos got word that the Chamber of Deputies had refused to declare his seat vacant he took his family home. As a deputy he would be immune to arrest.

He was re-elected to congress by an even larger majority in 1958. Reformist sentiment was strong. This was the year when in scornful protest a hundred thousand people in a state election in São Paulo wrote in on their ballots the name of Cacareco, a rhinoceros in the city zoo that was a great favorite with the schoolchildren.

The Politics of the Broom

Kubitschek proved an energetic President. He had the knack of getting cooperation out of the most diverse factions. Political bitterness diminished during his sixyear term. Industrial growth was immense.

As a native of an inland state he was convinced of the need to move the federal capital to the central plateau. Brasília was a colossal achievement, but it proved a colossally expensive achievement.

All the economic ills which resulted from the narrow

views of the nationalists, and from the highhanded neglect of fiscal problems that had been the rule for years, began to come home to roost. The loss of value of the cruzeiro and the daily rise in the cost of living became the dominant facts in Brazilian life.

Jânio Quadros, with the assistance of sound economic advisors and, particularly, of Carvalho Pinto, the hardworking fiscal expert who was to succeed him as governor, had made good his promise to put the finances of the wealthy state of São Paulo back in order. When he announced his presidential candidacy to succeed Juscelino Kubitschek, the voters believed he would do the same thing for the federal government. His emblem was still the new broom. As a mass meeting orator he had no rival. No one paid any attention to stories of his drinking, of his emotional instability, of the passes he made at nubile young women who found themselves alone in his office. He aroused overwhelming enthusiasm. He was elected President by six million votes.

By a quirk in the constitution the Vice-President could seek re-election, though the President could not. In spite of a split in the labor vote João Goulart marshaled enough of Vargas' old following to become Vice-President once more.

The same hopes for a thoroughgoing reform of the government that carried Jânio Quadros into the Palace of the Dawn at Brasília, carried Carlos Lacerda into the governorship of the new state of Guanabara. Next to the presidency, being governor of Guanabara was the toughest political assignment in Brazil.

The preceding administration had been so taken up with Brasília that the beautiful old capital was left in the doldrums. The city kept growing. New quarters were springing up in every nook of the difficult terrain between the bay of Guanabara on one side and the lagoon on the other. The close-packed buildings were hemmed in everywhere by the tooth-shaped basalt peaks that form the chief beauty of the city's landscape. Transportation was in a snarl. A complete new highway system was needed. Electric light, power, water were insufficient. The telephone service was years behind the times. The sewers mostly dated from the mid-nineteenth century when Rio was rated as having one of the best systems in the world. Even the handsomest residential quarters were flanked by hillside slums, the famous favelas. By this time almost a million squatters lived in these shantytowns without policing or public services of any kind. The condition of Rio would have been a challenge to a man who had spent his life in public administration.

To the amazement of friend and foe, Governor Lacerda, after a little preliminary fumbling, developed one of the most efficient administrations the city had ever seen. He collected about him a group of townplanners and architects and engineers and laid plans for new electric light plants, for a new water supply, for renovating the sewerage system and for dealing with a long list of what he called skeletons, projects started by previous administrations that had been halted for lack of funds. When the Alliance for Progress came along he eagerly took advantage of American money. He announced his administration's aim to "make Rio once more the Marvelous City."

"Oh, marvelous city," went a popular song. "By day we lack water, and by night we lack light."

The President Breaker

It was at Jânio Quadros' suggestion that Carlos Lacerda ran for the governorship of Guanabara. During the early months of Quadros' presidency the two men continued to see eye to eye. Quadros' first administrative reforms had Lacerda's hearty approval. The governor's plan was to keep pace in his local administration with the President's reform of the federal government.

The trouble that began to develop between them stemmed from the fact that the problems Quadros had to meet at Brasília were much tougher than the problems he had coped with in São Paulo. There he had the advantage of able collaborators, since the city and state of São Paulo had for years enjoyed the most competent administration in Brazil. In São Paulo the new broom could be placed in the hands of men who knew how to use it.

In Brasília everything was chaotic. The capital city had been only recently inaugurated. More than half the government offices were still in Rio. Politicians, and particularly their wives and families, balked at exchanging the familiar amenities of the old capital for the windswept immensities of bare red clay and the dust of construction work of the fantastic new city on the plateau five hundred miles inland. Niemeyer's new congress building was striking to behold but inconvenient to operate. Even when the President could coax enough senators and deputies out to Brasília for a quorum he found it hard to keep their minds on constructive legislation. He was confronted by the fact that running a vast sprawling nation, where the problems of government were different in each different region, was a far more exacting task than acting the spellbinder as figurehead for that nation's best organized state. Failure stared him in the face.

Lacerda now says that Jânio was a charlatan all along. He points out his slovenly working habits, his lack of education, that his only reading had been some Shakespeare and a little Zola. His taste in art Lacerda found atrocious. Though immensely clever at picking ideas out of other men's mouths, Jânio, says Lacerda, always lacked the inner cohesion needed to face adversity. Still he can't help admitting that at the time of Jânio's inauguration, like millions of other Brazilians, he expected a miracle.

Unable to cope with the complications of reforming the federal government, Quadros began to listen to advisers who brought up the parallel of Fidel Castro in Cuba. Castro wasn't plagued with a recalcitrant congress, with a faultfinding press or with powerful financial interests all tugging in different directions. Castro was having it all his own way. Instead of piecemeal reform, maybe Brazil needed a Castro-type revolution. Jânio's gift for swaying the crowd was equal to Fidel's. With dictatorial powers he could really use his new broom.

Quadros wanted Lacerda's help in this half formulated enterprise. Members of his administration turned up in Rio, suggesting that Lacerda's own work would be easier if the President and the state governors had more power. Lacerda's answer was that Quadros had all the power he needed. He had the prestige. He had the backing of the whole population. What he must do was present an itemized program to congress. Popular clamor would do the rest.

Gradually it dawned on Lacerda that Quadros had no program to offer. He wanted power first. The program could wait. The newspapers were full of the handsome reception the President was giving to Fidel Castro's mission to Brazil.

The old watchdog of democracy was aroused. He talked with other state governors and federal senators. He became convinced that something unhealthy was brewing at Brasília.

Although it was second nature to Lacerda to make his every thought public in his newspaper or on the air, he kept his doubts to himself until at last he could contain himself no longer; he must have it out with President Quadros.

Quadros was in Brasília. His wife, Dona Elvá de Quadros, whom Lacerda speaks of as a really nice sensible woman, was in Rio. Lacerda went to see her at the presidential residence and explained to her that he had to have a quiet talk with her husband. The answer was an invitation to dine that same night and the appearance of the President's jet to transport Governor Lacerda to Brasília.

It was from the President's military attaché, who met him

at the airport, that Lacerda learned that Quadros had just given the most important Brazilian decoration to Castro's chief assistant, "Ché" Guevara. The President's household was caught by surprise.

Sensing that he was in for a rough time Lacerda sent his secretary to engage a room at the hotel and proceeded to the palace. There he was met by someone he described as "a sort of Gregório" who took his little black overnight case and showed him to a suite. The first sour note was that the President had already dined. Governor Lacerda dined alone.

Then President Quadros suddenly put in an appearance. He greeted Lacerda warmly and gave him a friendly hug. It was obvious that he had had a few drinks. Lacerda immediately started to tell him of his doubts and suspicions. He asked for an explanation. He said he didn't want to go back to his days of wild attacks but he owed something to his voters and to the country. He explained that he couldn't go along with Jânio's pro-Castro foreign policy. Maybe he'd better resign as governor. The country had a right to a little peace and quiet.

He added that he had personal reasons too. When he took over the governorship he had turned his newspaper over to his son Sérgio. The boy was having a hard time. He didn't want him to meet failure so young. Jânio gave Lacerda a sharp look and cried out that if it was money he needed for his newspaper he would attend to that.

Lacerda answered that he didn't want money. His newspaper could take care of itself. He wanted some assurance that Jânio Quadros wasn't trying to behave like Fidel Castro.

Quadros is a smallish man with a Charlie Chaplin mustache. Lacerda, who had always been on good terms with him, tried to kid him: Come now he wasn't Charles de Gaulle.

"Let's go to the movies," said Jânio.

Seeing movies every night had become an obsession with

him. The big hall in the palace was rigged up with a motion picture screen. There were tables piled with sausages and cold meats, bowls of popcorn, beer and whiskey bottles. Quadros had the reputation of having a good head for liquor, but by this time he was showing it.

They started with a serious picture but the President shouted that he wanted something funny. He called for Jerry Lewis. He didn't like Jerry Lewis and switched to a Western. He was a great fan of Westerns.

In the middle of the reel the President went to the phone. He came back and told Lacerda he wanted him to confer with two of his ministers who were having a private talk in a room at the hotel.

When Lacerda reached the hotel all the ministers would talk about was some articles Lacerda had written in the period after Vargas' suicide, suggesting that elections be postponed. Why didn't he favor direct action now? Lacerda told them that the situation today was very different. He added that he was planning to resign his governorship since he could not go along with the national administration. He would try to keep his opinions to himself to give them a free hand.

After that, he returned to the palace, under the impression that he'd been invited to spend the night there. At the entrance he was met by the doorman who handed him his little black bag. The doorman intimated he'd better go to the hotel.

Lacerda tells of the ride back to the hotel as one of the worst moments of his life. He was oppressed by the vast loneliness of the unfinished city, the great buildings with nobody in them, the ghost town look. There was a Nazi atmosphere about the crazy scene at the palace, the incoherence, the drinking, the silly movie. From his hotel room he called up one of the ministers he'd been talking to before. The minister came to his room. They argued until four in the morning.

Lacerda insisted that this sort of thing couldn't go on. It was the Stalin way of running a country. The minister told him the President said to go to hell.

Lacerda flew back to Rio the next day. A couple of days later he had a date to lecture to university students in São Paulo. He tried to make a figurative speech as a warning to Jânio. An organized group kept interrupting him, shouting, *"Jânio sim, Lacerda não."*

This was for Lacerda a period of terrible indecision. He couldn't sleep nights. Then on August 24, the anniversary of the downfall of Getúlio Vargas, he made up his mind. That night he spoke to the nation over TV. He told the whole story of the trip to Brasília, his frustration, the efforts to induce him to fall in with Jânio's plans. "The man we elected doesn't want to be President, he wants to be dictator."

Next day Jânio Quadros resigned. With his resignation he gave out a confused statement that hidden interests at home and abroad were sabotaging his program. He may have thought that a wave of popular outbursts would force the congress to ask him to reconsider his resignation. There was no such outburst. A few months later Adhemar de Barros, who is not lacking in humor, announced on television that he didn't know about the sinister domestic interests that had ruined Quadros' program, but he could name the foreign interests. They were Haig & Haig, Teacher's, Johnnie Walker, and so forth.

Quadros' resignation left João Goulart, Vargas' political heir, the President of Brazil. All parties, except for the left wing of labor and the Communists, were thrown into dismay. Congress, under the influence of the Democratic Union, immediately started tinkering with the constitution. The President was shorn of his powers. The executive power was placed in the hands of a Prime Minister responsible to the Chamber of Deputies.

Politically the period between Quadros' resignation in the summer of '61 and the October elections in the fall of '62 was the story of a continuous tug of war between the leaders of the Democratic Union, who wanted ministerial government, and the Labor Party men who wanted full presidential powers restored to their leader. National administration was at a stalemate, with the result that no constructive legislation could be passed. Inflation went unchecked. The cost of living soared. In spite of occasional hikes in the minimum wage, the middle classes were pinched and working people's families went hungry. In the hinterlands the unemployed starved.

The Reactionary Governor of Guanabara

After his crucial television speech Lacerda says he was at last able to sleep soundly in his bed. He awoke to a chorus of praise and vituperation. Jânio Quadros' resignation was as great a shock to the Brazilian electorate as Vargas' suicide. Men and women of all levels of society had placed their hopes in his hands. The first reaction was of despair.

The conservative newspapers came around to the view that, shocking as it was, Lacerda's unmasking of Quadros saved Brazilian democracy. The leftwing press, led by the dashingly edited *Ultima Hora* with its nationwide circulation, claimed that having brought about Vargas' death the reactionary governor of Guanabara had now deprived the country of the services of its most dedicated reformer. The man was a monster. Some people have been called kingmakers. Lacerda was the destroyer of presidents.

No man loves a fight more. Breathing deep of the dust of battle Lacerda threw himself into an almost nightly vendetta over television with the supporters of President Goulart. As the campaign for the congressional elections of 1962 neared its climax, he seemed to foreign observers to be engaged in a sort of hand to hand combat over the airwaves with Leonel Brizola, the President's brotherinlaw.

Brizola was nearing the end of his term as governor of Rio Grande do Sul. In spite of the backing of some of Vargas' henchmen in the state which had been the center of the old dictator's political web, his administration had been so unpopular that he was facing a voters' revolt at home. By following the anti-American line in Guanabara, where there was a compact Communist-inspired vote, he would be sure of election to the Chamber of Deputies. By bearding Lacerda in his own citystate he could hope to win national leadership of the Brazilian Labor Party.

So long as he was governor of Rio Grande do Sul, Brizola could use other weapons than oratory. A severe drought had resulted in a scarcity of rice and beans throughout the northern and central part of Brazil. Rio Grande do Sul had a surplus. Brizola could use his control of his home state's export of vital foods to cut off supplies from Guanabara. Beans and rice are basic articles in the diet of all classes in Brazil. The rich can eat other things. If the poor can't get beans they go hungry. The sight of long queues waiting for beans and rice in markets and foodstores was a more cogent argument against Lacerda's administration than all the oratory in the world.

While Brizola, supported by an active political organization which controlled the flow of cash to labor unions and students' organizations, fought Lacerda over the air, his brotherinlaw's administration in Brasília made life as hard as possible for the state of Guanabara. Everything the federal government could do was done to sabotage Lacerda's program.

It was a mighty struggle. Lacerda's capacity for work has always been prodigious. While he carried on the debate with Brizola in almost nightly television appearances, he worked all day superintending every detail of his rebuilding of Rio. He wore out secretaries and assistants. He had to prove to himself and to the world that his plans for the "marvelous city" were not just politicians' talk. He had to show results that the voters could see.

As governor he lives on the top floor of an old apartment house facing the bay in a somewhat rundown residential section known as Flamengo Beach. First thing in the morning he's out on the balcony looking down to see how the work is going on one of his favorite projects.

Early in his governorship he took steps to insure the public use of a large area of made land through which the new four-lane highway runs from the downtown district out along the bay shore to Copacabana and the new seabeach suburbs. He wants to develop this region into a park which will surpass in beauty the old parks that are part of the imperial heritage, and, at the same time furnish playgrounds, small boat harbors, soccerfields and beach facilities for the city's growing population.

To superintend the project he appointed a committee under the active management of his old friend Lota de Macedo Soares. As a great hostess Dona Lota numbered among her personal cronies many of the world's best architects and sculptors and townplanners. A small woman in black striped pants, she drives them with fair words, but she drives them hard. She has Burle Marx, Brazil's most internationally admired landscape architect, doing the overall design and has dragged in the best talent in the country to help. Many of them work without pay. They'll tell you that not a tree is planted, nor a stretch of shrubbery set in position which escapes the governor's early morning gaze. Usually he's after Dona Lota on the phone before eight o'clock to find out why some part of the work isn't going along faster.

Next, after a couple of early morning hours at his administrative office, Governor Lacerda will be out on his rounds to see for himself. He has to see and be seen. The people must be made to know he's working for them.

First he'll turn up at a hilltop favela, climbing the goat-paths with a springy step while a subordinate pants after him with a bundle of documents. The documents are to declare the hill expropriated by right of eminent domain from the original owners. The owners haven't been getting any profits anyway as they are helpless to evict the squatters and in some cases they are compensated by special privileges as to zoning and building heights in the more accessible sections of their land.

Lacerda's program for the squatters is twofold. Where the land must be used for other construction, they are offered cheap substitute housing in rows of small dwellings which, though not luxurious, are at least better than the hovels they will be leaving. In the majority of cases it is not practical to move the people out. Then the city services bring in light and water. Something is done about sewage. Receptacles are set up for garbage where trucks can reach them. The governor furnishes cement, lumber, and technical help for these projects, but the heavy work is done by the faveladwellers themselves.

Lacerda is delighted by the success in the favelas of the institution of mutirão, mutual help. Since most of the squatters are recent immigrants from the backlands they are used to the old peasant system. If a man is building a house the neighbors pitch in to help. They work the same way in the favelas. The governor's plan is to give the squatters title to the little plots they have already built their houses on, and gradually to draw them into the benefits and responsibilities of citizenship. "We want them to feel," he says, "that they are regular people . . . just like anybody else."

Leaving the favela the governor will pick up his chief engineer and visit the excavations where they are laying a new sewer, or check on the work on the tunnels being drilled

through the mountains for the new water supply, which is to
be chlorinated and treated with fluorine at the source. Then
he'll dedicate a clinic that is part of his program for renovating the obsolete hospitals, or cut the tape on a new thoroughfare designed to alleviate some of Rio's unending traffic jam.
Almost daily he opens a school. There are so many new schools
he's run out of names for them and asks his visitors to make
lists of suggestions. Next it's a viaduct or the beginning of a
great traffic tunnel to link an isolated part of the city into the
highway system.

He seems to carry all the details in his head. He gives the
impression of knowing more about each project than the men
in charge. Though he's death on incompetence, he keeps the
enthusiasm of his staff at a high pitch. Good work is immediately recognized. "I wouldn't have believed it," said one of
Lacerda's oldest friends, a lawyer who had helped him set up
his newspaper fifteen years before. "We thought of him as
the editorial writer, the fearless orator. To have him turn into
an administrator is the surprise of the century . . . Why,
he's actually happy in administration."

Brazil is a land of thoroughgoing social democracy. A public man has to be open to anybody who wants to talk to him.
On his rounds Lacerda has to be ready with a little speech
for every occasion. Humorous hardhitting casual discourses
come easy as breathing. Everywhere the crowd presses around
him. He seems to have time for everyone, for old women
whose sons are in trouble, for a lame man who can't get into
a hospital, for a young man who wants him to start a school
for television technicians. Doctors, engineers, hospital nurses,
all whisper their problems in his ear. By night the men on his
staff are worn out. Governor Lacerda is still ready to talk with
a foreign visitor, or to dine with a group of American students.

Tonight a couple of the students have managed to get lost. At going home time between five and seven in Rio taxis can't be found. Buses and trolleys are packed tight as sardinetins. We sit waiting on a sofa in the livingroom. In spite of his punishing schedule the governor shows no sign of impatience.

He does admit to having a bad cold. Though his voice is hoarse his talk flows on. He has an extraordinary flow of words in Portuguese and in English. He starts to tell about the loneliness of his position. It is the custom in Brazil for a public man to find jobs for all his friends and relatives. Lacerda has kept them at arm's length. He sees nothing else to do. This has done him more harm than anything. So many people who used to be fond of him now think he's a terrible fellow.

There are other things he'd like to do, other things than fighting Communists and fellowtravelers, he'd like to take time off to write a novel. He'd like to be Minister of Education in a federal administration he had confidence in, or ambassador to Washington. He feels he knows Washington well enough to get past the pundits and the knowitall columnists and to explain Brazil to the American people in Brazilian terms.

The phone rings. A secretary comes in to announce that the lost students are on their way.

We go down in the elevator. Two uniformed militiamen who guard the front door stiffen to salute. We get into the governor's old model black car. Still no students. It's against the traffic rules to park in front of the apartment house so Lacerda tells the chauffeur to drive around the corner. We wait in a dark and solitary street.

There's no bodyguard, only the little chauffeur.

This is at the height of the political war. A few days before, Lacerda read off the list of Moscow-trained Communists in key posts in Goulart's administration. The answer was a demand that the federal government "intervene" in Guanabara. "Intervention" was Vargas' way of removing uncooperative state governors. Lacerda replied that he had been legally elected by the people of the state and if they tried to take him out of his office they would take him out dead.

There have been a few small riots between Lacerda supporters and Brizola's people. Brizola is in town. When he addresses a public meeting he has a military bodyguard. There have been new rumors of threats against Lacerda's life.

The minutes drag on. We three are alone in the dark empty street. It is obvious that the thought of personal danger never crosses Lacerda's mind. While he chats cheerfully of one thing and another part of his brain is busy planning what he is going to say later tonight after dinner when he appears on TV. He grumbles a little about Brochado da Rocha, Goulart's Prime Minister. As a lawyer in Rio Grande do Sul he had a good reputation, but as a politician he's proved an absolute ninny. Though a man of moderate opinions Lacerda says he's turned to putty in the hands of the Communists.

After twenty minutes the American students appear. They are full of apologies, with bright shiny faces. Lacerda seems happy airing his American slang. He's happy having the Americans there though he knows very well that this is one campaign when contact with an American is a liability. Nobody defends the Alliance for Progress. Yankeebaiting is the order of the day. Lacerda's never been a man to give in before popular clamor. We all eat dinner at the yachtclub very much in the public eye. Afterwards he goes off to the television station to lash at his enemies in a twohour speech.

One, Two, and Three, Cried the Count of Montecristo

When Lacerda went on the air and called Brochado da Rocha the cheerful *vivandière* of the Goulart regime, that hitherto rather colorless politician blew his top. At the next cabinet meeting he threatened to resign as Prime Minister unless Lacerda were removed as Governor of Guanabara. He cried out passionately that he would not be able to look his children in the eye if he went home without some punishment for Lacerda. The leftwing press went into an uproar. However, military influences made themselves felt in Brasília. Brochado da Rocha had to be satisfied with a vote of censure on Lacerda by the council of ministers.

Juscelino Kubitschek had been busy rebuilding his old coalition between Goulart's party and his Social Democrats. His aim was seemingly to strengthen the right wing of the Labor Party and to wean the President away from Brizola and the Communist apparatus. Now he had to go flying to Brasília to apply the healing oil. He had already come out for a return of full powers to the presidency. Why not? He was planning to be President again himself. He could appeal with some authority to João Goulart not to let the situation get out of hand.

Not long after, in a reshuffling of the Cabinet to bring it more in line with Goulart's ambitions, Brochado da Rocha was forced out. He went home to his state capital at Pôrto Alegre and a few days later was taken with a cerebral hemorrhage and went to bed and died.

The Communist-inspired press attacked Lacerda as a murderer. He was a Lucifer of reaction. He was plotting with American imperialists. Subsidized by American funds he had again brought about the death of an eminent Brazilian statesman. Vargas dead, Quadros ruined, and now Brochado da Rocha. The nation must be rid of this sinister influence.

Postmortem

In spite of the clamor the elections passed off in peace and quiet on October 7. Just before election day Lacerda obtained a two months' leave of absence from his legislature to go to

Europe to study European subway systems. If he could start the construction of a subway while his governorship lasted he would have accomplished one more benefit for his "marvelous city." Already he could point out that the rate of new industrial investment in Guanabara had for the first time surpassed the rate in São Paulo.

The governor needed a rest indeed. Weeks and weeks of working eighteen hours a day had broken down even his robust health. The cold which had troubled him for weeks went to the brink of pneumonia before his doctor put him to bed. Candidates friendly to his policies had to finish their campaigns with little help from their leader.

The election returns, like those in similar elections held in the United States a month later, could be interpreted almost any way you wanted them. Communist-supported candidates won and anti-Communists won. The commentators however did point out that for Brazil it was a democratic victory. The forms of democracy were rigorously observed. There was no violence or intimidation at the polls and even very little talk of corruption. The turnout was large.

On account of the proportional system of representation it took a very long time to count the votes. The number of candidates for office was everywhere staggering. This meant a scattering of the independent vote which was an advantage to politicians with wellorganized machines.

In Guanabara, Lacerda's enemy Brizola was elected deputy by the largest vote on record. Anti-Americanism paid off. Lacerda's friends carried the state legislature but lost the vice governorship, which would mean difficulties for the governor during the rest of his term. The Alliance for Progress proved a liability.

In Pernambuco, the northeastern state where such efforts had been made by the Catholic Church and by influences from the United States to undercut the Communist peasant leagues, Miguel Arraes, the Communist-supported candidate won the governorship by a small margin. His campaign was largely financed by Brazil's second richest man, a manufacturer from São Paulo named Ermírio de Moraes. Moraes himself, who took the precaution of hiring every taxicab in the state capital of Recife to carry his voters to the polls on election day, went to the federal senate. These developments were a severe blow to Washington's hopes for an Alliance for Progress in Brazil.

However, in the key state of São Paulo the story was entirely different. Jânio Quadros tried for a political comeback and was defeated by his old enemy Adhemar de Barros, whose campaign was frankly directed against Communist and Castro influences. In President Goulart's own state of Rio Grande do Sul the voters made a clean sweep of his brotherinlaw Brizola's supporters. Menighetti, a conservative who had opposed Brizola's seizure of the American public utilities, was elected by a large majority. When news came of Brizola's election to the Chamber from Guanabara streamers appeared across the streets of Pôrto Alegre reading THANK YOU CARIO-CAS.

The Uniao Nacional Democratico came out badly. For a while it looked as if the chief beneficiary of the 1962 elections might be Juscelino Kubitschek, who wasn't running for any office at all. Certainly his position was improved as a contender for presidential nomination by the Social Democrats in 1965, but at the same time the figure of the present governor of Minas Gerais, Magelhães Pinto, began to loom as presidential timber. It is too early to say whether Lacerda has lost political prestige. This isn't his first political reverse. Growing enthusiasm for his presidential candidacy in 1965 is reported from São Paulo. At fortyeight he is just reaching political maturity. His is the most compelling presence on Brazilian television. He somehow finds words every voter can understand to explain the difference between the reorganization of society under freedom and the Communist or Castro way. The direct approach, the straight talk, the burning dedication of the dark eyes behind the shellrimmed glasses still hold his audiences spellbound.

Friends tell you laughingly about his European "vacation." Not an idle moment. In Paris he spent his time negotiating a deal with a French concern to install a subway in Rio which is to be financed largely by French funds. In West Germany he contracted for a hospital. He is not known to have done any work during the week he spent in Sicily. On the steamboat back from Italy he whiled away his time preparing a volume of his speeches for publication, and translating a Broadway play, *Come Blow Your Horn*, which he had found amusing one night in New York, from English into Portuguese for production in Rio.

VIII

THE UNEASY NORTHEAST

(meditations out of a traveler's notebook)

Boa Viajem, Recife,
September 13, 1962

The name of the beach means "pleasant journey." It brings up a picture of people riding out from the city in the old days to wave to their friends tacking out from the harbor entrance on sailing ships into the onshore breeze. I don't find the hotel as pleasant as it seemed when I was there with my wife and daughter four years ago; rebuilt and modernized, it lacks the rustic air it had. Maybe it's that my family has gone back to the States. There's been an immense amount of building. The beach has taken on a standardized resort look.

The fishermen have been chased away. Watching their *jangadas* was one of the real pleasures of our stay in Recife four years ago.

The *jangada* is a boatshaped raft made of logs of various light woods. The fishermen push them out in the morning over the heavy surf. Using a lateentype sail they cruise far out into the ocean. They fish with casting nets and hook and line. They steer with a paddle and with moveable leeboards pushed down between the logs, like on the *Kon-Tiki*. They are awash most of the time. We never did get to go out on one but it was a constant pleasure to follow their skillful navigation, tacking back and forth into the wind; and then the return in the afternoon running before the wind through gaps in the black reef that gave its name to this capital city of the ancient sugar state of Pernambuco, and back through the surf onto the beach.

The fishermen stored their gear in neatly made shelters of plaited palmleaves, up under the endlessly swaying rustling coconut palms. The catches they brought ashore in their deep baskets seemed pathetically small. These waters are not rich in fish.

For bathing, the sea is as delicious as ever.

Drying off in the mild late sun in the salt breeze that was almost cool—the season here is early spring: I've seen peachtrees in bloom—I felt a sudden gush of a very Portuguese state of mind: *saudades*. The *Pequeno Dictionário Brasileiro da Língua Portuguêsa* describes saudades, rather lyrically I thought, as "the sad and suave remembrance of persons or things distant or gone."

Four years ago we all enjoyed ourselves particularly on this beach. The surf was just right. The reef cuts the force of the waves.

There are landcrabs if you watch for them. They have a ghostly way of being gone before you see them, set high off the ground on spiderlegs like harness racers.

Gilberto Freyre was at his house in Apipucos. He played host for us for an entire day. It was like living a chapter of *Casa Grande e Senzala*. He took us out to lunch in the country at an ancient sugar plantation. The sugarmill wasn't working any more, and the young couple who entertained us, pleasant as they were, were like young couples with artistic tastes you might meet anywhere in the world, but somehow Freyre managed to evoke the sugarmill and the people who'd lived there through the years. He made us feel its history and its folklore . . . in depth through the years.

It was a day of semitropical beauty you could hardly believe: blue sky sprinkled, as if with confetti, with little halcyon clouds tinted with lavender and primrose and faintest brick color. The cane was a very lightgreen; the mangoes the very darkest green etched in black. In the shimmering sunlight every tree was a different green. There were sheep, and a duck-pond and geese, and cattle in a distant pasture. Country people on scrubby little horses passed along a country lane. Their straw hats, their clothes had a distinctive air. Even their dogs had a Pernambuco look.

The lunch tasted incredibly good. We ate a great deal and drank a great deal. Afterwards Freyre produced a pair of guitar-players. They sang what is called a *desafio*, a challenge. One man makes up a couplet and sings it and the other caps it. In between they keep the guitar strings throbbing. The whole thing is extemporary. The couplets deal with everything from national politics to the private lives of people in the audience. Everybody is kidded. The guitarists kid each other. The audience applauds a successful crack. For the rest of the day wherever we went the guitarists went with us. They gave a great performance.

In the afternoon we drove through farms and plantations on our way back to Freyre's house. We drank plenty and talked plenty. We were on the crest of the wave. We dined at the house of a Recife politician. Again the food was much too good. The desafio was going great guns. Afterwards our tireless friends went on to a nightclub, but we, pleading our daughter's tender years, went back to the Hotel Boa Viajem and to the salty night breeze rustling through the palms and the sound of the surf . . . Saudades.

This time four years later, the weather's threatening. The city of Recife has grown skyscrapers from every seam. It looks as if it had doubled in population. No place to park a car. The old town on the island has lost its quaint Dutch look.

I miss old buildings I had remembered. If it weren't that my friends the Ellebys put me up in their house made lively by their children, I'd be feeling depressed indeed.

Among the Americans I find a good deal of gloom. The Alliance for Progress seems stalled. Among the Department of Agriculture people to be sure there's talk of a real breakthrough in rainforest agriculture. If it's true it's the most exciting news since chloroquin. So much to be done . . . if it weren't for the Communists.

For the first time, in all my batting around Brazil, walking with a group of Americans at lunchtime into a restaurant, I see real hostility in the faces of the people at the other tables.

The people who for want of a better word we call intellectuals are subject to obsessions the world over. The anti-McCarthyism of the collegiate and bureaucratic classes in the States became an obsession. In Brazil anti-Americanism may be becoming the current obsession of the intellectuals.

In São Paulo, at the lawschool at the old university, I tried to have it out with a group of law students. Personally they couldn't have been more cordial, but their prejudice stuck out like a sore thumb. First they brought up, as everybody does, our discrimination against Negroes in the South, but they seemed to see the point when I explained that three or four southern states constituted a small part of the population of the United States and that even there an effort was being made. (I might have added that the average southern Negro gets a whole lot better break than a workingman in Brazil.) Why was it, one young man who had been to Los Angeles, insisted, that everybody born north of the Rio Grande considered himself better than anybody born south of it. I pointed out that it was a natural human failing to think of your own group as being tops. The *paulistas* were famous for that. They laughed. They really had me when they began to ask questions about American writers. They knew Faulkner and Hem-

ingway and Salinger and Cummings. Their questions showed
thought and information. I kept thinking: suppose I were
talking to a group of students back home; they wouldn't even
know whether Brazilians wrote Spanish or Portuguese. Perhaps
it's our ignorance that galls them so.

It seemed strange to me that they never mentioned the Bay
of Pigs. Politeness, maybe.

I may be wrong, maybe I haven't talked to enough of them;
but I don't seem to find anti-American prejudice among
working people. If they know Americans at all they like them,
perhaps because we tend to be more openhanded towards
working people than the Brazilians. Better wages. The com-
plaint of the housewives is that Americans spoil their maids.
The North American idea that people who do manual work
should for that very reason get a little better than fair and
equal treatment has made little progress in the southern continent. Of course a lot of Brazilian working people vote the
pro-Communist and anti-American tickets. They have to vote
the way the labor bosses tell them to. It's a question of bread
and butter. They repeat the Communist slogans without paying much attention to them. If they read, they do believe to
a certain extent what they read in *Ultima Hora*, but they
don't seem to feel the hatred the journalists feel who write in
it. The working people are too busy trying to get a square
meal, a roof over their heads, a few clothes for the children,
and the price of a soccer game Sunday.

Modern Communism, what in Brazil you might call the
Fidel Castro mentality, is an obsession of the intellectuals.
Politics is, after all, the ladder to success. In recent years university students here have given a great deal more time to
politics than to study or technical training. Whether they
were justified or not, student strikes have paralyzed higher education. Dedication to knowledge: scholarship is almost forgotten as a way of life. Many students, whether Communist
or anti-Communist, throw all their energy into the political

activities of the student organizations. Being a student has become a profession.

The anti-Communists mostly have to work gratis. The Communists get paid in various ways; traveling expenses to meetings, travel to Cuba or the Soviet Union, board and lodging during indoctrination courses. If they write articles they are sure to get them published. A writer who doesn't offend the Communists finds his books get a good press. There are Communist claques in the publishing houses and in the newspapers. It's much easier to swim with the tide than against it.

The last thing the young Brazilians who graduate from the university want to do is to engage in manual labor. We have a similar state of mind developing in the United States, but with us the old Protestant tradition of the nobility of work still has a certain strength. The career they look forward to is officeholding, and Communism looms ahead as the officeholder's paradise. Even in opposition and illegality the Party offers careers to its adherents. The magic of the Marxist ideology turns careerism into altruism. The student leaders think of themselves as dedicated idealists.

The Communists are struggling against imperialism and exploitation: how can an idealist oppose them? The Communist imperialism and Communist exploitation they read about in the newspapers doesn't impress them. The Berlin wall; they shrug it off. The development of the demagoguery of revolution in Mexico should have proved a corrective, but the lesson has been lost.

Of course the nationalists have a story, in Brazil as they did in Mexico. Though great sectors of industry are now wholly or partly in Brazilian hands, some foreign utilities are still owned abroad. Fear of nationalization has inhibited improvements or even decent maintenance. Investment is at a standstill. In Rio there are people who have been waiting twenty years for a telephone. In trying to protect their stockholders the foreign boards of directors have thrown the Brazilian consumer to the wolves. As a result both consumers and stockholders have lost out. The financial managers can't seem to think of anything except how to get their companies bailed out by the American taxpayer when expropriation finally comes.

It is a sorry end to the history of American and European investment in South America, which produced so many engineering marvels in its day. It is a situation made to order for Communist propaganda.

With Goulart's administration in charge of the federal government, Brazilian Communism seems to be entering its heyday. The tragic thing to me is that the Marxist theory has nothing to offer that can solve the country's problems. The most pressing need is to grow enough food to feed the population. The world 'over, Marxism has failed to produce food. Brazil's spreading frontier demands individual initiative. All Communism has to offer is increased power to a bureaucracy which has already proved its incompetence. With a government that can't keep the employees from stealing the stamps off the letters in the postoffice, the rational thing you would think would be to call for less rather than more power for the politicians.

When you come to think of it, maybe the Communists and near Communists are no more powerful in Brazil than they are in the United States. There's nothing in the history of Brazilian relations with the spreading Soviet power as disturbingly illogical as the behavior of various administrations in Washington. The Brazilian press suffers from none of the inhibitions against clear thinking that muddy the mental processes of the American liberals. The Rio and São Paulo newspapers are as vigorous and varied and scurrilous and satirical and generally rambunctious as the American newspapers used to be in their salad days before schools of journalism and the Newspaper Guild and the breakdown of competition. The best pens are in the anti-Communist camp. "How the hell," I said to myself, "can we ask the Brazilians to follow our leadership when there isn't any?"

In spite of the soothing roar of the surf on Pleasant Journey beach, none of these reflections made for sound sleeping.

Natal, the Governor's Guesthouse,
September 14

Doug Elleby drove me up from Recife in a jeep. At breakfast the Recife newspapers were full of Brochado da Rocha's resignation as Prime Minister. The unions, which are under the direct control of President Goulart's Ministry of Labor, are threatening a general strike if the congress doesn't speed measures for a return to "presidentialism." That's a pitch of labor demagogy we haven't yet quite reached in the United States.

Leaving Recife the first thing that struck me was the road. Four years ago nobody would have dreamed of trying to drive from Recife to Natal, even in a jeep. We skirt Olinda on a firstrate wellgraded highway. A glimpse of the faded tiled roofs and the belfries of the ancient Dutch capital makes me wish I had time for one more look at the beautiful Portuguese tilework and the fine arches of the old convents there. North of Olinda we drive through a beautiful rolling green country. The dark sculptured mango trees give the country a landscaped look. The houses are stucco on adobe with red and yellow tile roofs. They seem comfortable. This is oniongrowing country and fairly prosperous.

After an hour the trees grow smaller. The only cultivation is in the valleys. Fewer fruit trees and more sugar cane. After we cross the state line from Pernambuco into Paraíba we drive through a region of thorny underbrush interspersed with small gnarled trees. The road is graded but it hasn't been blacktopped yet. Parts are under construction. Eroding streams have taken deep bites out of the new raised causeways across bottomlands. Occasionally a washout almost cuts the road in two. No road for night driving.

A little more than two hours from Recife we reach João Pessoa which is the capital of the small state of Paraíba. It's a pleasant little yellowstucco city. The new quarters radiate along streets laid out like spokes of a wheel from a circular pond bordered with palms. The beach, studded with vast banyantrees, each tree a thicket by itself, opens in a halfmoon on a Nilegreen lagoon protected by a distant black reef where the surf spumes. Beyond the ocean is deepest indigo to the horizon. Jangadas skim back and forth in the fresh trade wind. Skinny sunblackened men wade with shrimpnets in the shallows. The waiter who serves us a beer under the trees points out that the impressivelooking promontory to the south of the lagoon is the easternmost point of Brazil, less than 35° west of Greenwich.

Leaving town down a cobbled hill we have a lovely view of a little port on the river, rusty small steamboats, ancient sailingships and a great stretch of salt marshes behind. We speed along the straight cement road which leads to Campina Grande, the most important town in Paraíba. It is too far out of our way; so we turn north on a dirt road so as to drive through Sapé.

Sapé is reputed to be one of the centers of Julião's *Ligas Camponêsas*. Julião is a landowner from Pernambuco who at one time had pretentions towards literature. Under the influence of Communist activists he has organized peasant leagues which are said to receive arms and guerrilla warfare training through agents of Fidel Castro. Their program is for the tenants to take over the land by force. It is quiet this morning. We did see one man with a rifle; and walls and buildings occasionally decorated with the hammer and sickle, and with VIVA CASTRO in brightblue paint.

His illwishers tell the story on Julião that when the peasants took him at his word and started to occupy his own estate he called in the Army to protect it. Could be; but it seems a little too pat.

What, you ask yourself, would you do in their place?

It's a hilly country with small patches of decent land, a little like the Piedmont region of North Carolina. We pass extensive plantations of pineapple, packingsheds with stacks of crates ready for shipment. Doug tells me that there's an active pineapplegrowers' cooperative in Sapé. They are trying to enlarge their export market to include the United States. Now their pineapples go to Europe or the Argentine.

Overpopulated. We pass through too many dusty little stone villages. The crumbling adobe huts have a company town look. People are poor all right. If I had to live there I'd feel rebellious too. But even driving through, it becomes fairly obvious that redistribution of the land won't solve the problem. There's not enough good land to go around. In North Carolina the solution was textile mills. Here it might be small industry. It might be resettlement on virgin lands to the west. Cutting the throats of the landlords isn't going to help.

It's so much easier to appeal to envy, hatred and malice than to work out rational solutions: therein lies the success of the Communist play for power.

The landlords in the Northeast are no bargain either. Many of them would rather die than give their tenants a break. The basic trouble is that there's not enough to go around. I was told the story of a man in Pernambuco who personally beat up one of his tenants for planting banana trees round his hut. I suppose the landlord thought that if the tenant had a few bananas to eat he wouldn't cut cane at the going rate. Still, if the politicians would only give them a chance the pineapplegrowers' cooperative might well do more to raise the standard of living around Sapé than the peasant leagues.

We cross into Rio Grande do Norte. Now the land is really poor but there are less people on it. The long rolling hills are shaped a little like the great green hills of Normandy, but they are sandy and arid. Scraggly vegetation under a flaming sun. In the valleys we see traces of abandoned sugar plantations. Here and there the stump of a brick chimney rises among the ruins of an old refinery. Even where there's still cultivation the cane has a starved look. There is a great deal of it. From one rise we look out into the shimmer of sunlight on enormous canefields, blue like the shimmer on a lake.

The first sign of Natal, the state capital, is a row of old U.S. radio masts left over from World War II sticking up from the top of a hill. Then there are military hangars, nicely painted airport buildings on a vast empty expanse of concrete landingstrips. We are driving on a hardtop road that is unmistakably American. To the right, bluffs jut into the misty blue ocean over great spuming purple rocks. The seabreeze is suddenly cool. The large seedylooking gray building is a hospital. Visiting Americans put up there, Doug Elleby says, by arrangement with the nuns, because the hotel is so horrible.

We stop off at the hotel in the center of town. An unappetizing dump. A few discouraged looking customers sit sweating in the lobby. Gin and tonic is available in the bar but no sandwiches. We've had no lunch. It's three in the afternoon and we are ravenous. All we can get to eat is some dried up strips of Dutch cheese. No bread.

A gentleman from the state government appears to take me to the guesthouse. Brazilian friends in Rio have arranged for the governor to take me along on a tour of the state starting tomorrow. I say goodby to my American escorts.

Aluísio Alves, a man of thirtynine who is present governor of Rio Grande do Norte, is, so it has been explained to me, one of the young men with a passion for social service who represent a new breed of Brazilian politician. It is this new breed of politician that will give the Communists a hard time.

He was born in Angicos, a little hamlet in the longstaple cotton region in the center of the state. He studied in Natal and took his law degree at the University of Alagoas in Maceió, an ancient city on the coast a hundred or so miles south of Recife. At twentyone, while still a student, he was elected federal deputy, one of the youngest on record. In Rio he became national secretary of the Democratic Union and a friend of Carlos Lacerda's. Along with Lacerda he was one of the founders of the *Tribuna da Imprensa* which he edited during Lacerda's exile. Since then there have been political differences between the two, particularly since Alves was elected governor of his home state in 1960 with Social Democrat backing.

On the way to the guesthouse I got the notion that—although possibly for political reasons the Alves administration was keeping Americans at arm's length—the American troops had left not too unpleasant memories behind them in Natal.

At the guesthouse I was ushered into a princely pink bedroom hung with mirrors and festooned with plush that looked out through shuttered windows on a garden on one side and an airy terrace on the other. In Brazil it's always a feast or a famine. The shower in the bathroom not only worked, but the water was hot. A shower was a godsend after all that dust. We'd arrived with half the state of Paraíba caked on our necks. I lunched in solitary splendor at a great oval table set as if for a state banquet.

Afterwards I was driven to the seat of government which the present incumbent has renamed Palacio da Esperanza (the Palace of Hope). Governor Alves is a showman. From the beginning of his campaign for the governorship he has used the green flag of hope as a trademark.

A green flag fluttered over the building and the official cars parked outside had green flags. Aluísio Alves makes a great play for the young. The government palace was as full of teenagers as Washington, D.C. during the Easter vacation. The central stairway swarmed with boys and girls. They chattered in the anterooms. There were so many youthful committees packed into the governor's office that you could hardly see his desk.

Aluísio Alves has, like so many Brazilians, the knack of looking younger than he is. He is a slender man with sunken cheeks. Except for his harassed air of a man in the middle of a political campaign he looks almost as youthful as the high-school kids all about him.

He has a brusque decisive manner. His Portuguese is so clear and sharp I can understand every word. In a flash he arranges an appointment with Bishop Sales whom I have asked to see. He tells off a young man from his secretariat to see that I get to the afternoon's *comicio*. He himself is up to his neck in appointments. He explains that he is not up for election. He is campaigning for a favorable legislature. His term has three more years to run.

José Augusto who has been detailed as my guide is a student of law. Right in Natal he's learned fluent English. He's too young to have learned it from the Americans. He's so younglooking I don't like to ask his age. He has plans for the diplomatic service. Itamarití. No, his secretarial work doesn't interfere with his studies. It is good practice. He'd like to go to the States, to perfect his English and to see. He almost got a fellowship but something went wrong. The man who was backing him died. He wishes it could be this year. Next year will be too late. He'll be training for the foreign service. Already he has the suave diplomat's manner, but under it you feel a somewhat steely personality. I'd bet that young man will go far.

The meeting was interesting. An enormous crowd packed a Y-shaped intersection of streets. Green bunting, signs, posters, campaign mottoes. Rockets sizzle up from the outskirts of the crowd to go bang overhead in the rosy sky of the swift twi-

light. Bats—or were they some kind of nighthawk?—flitter
overhead. Night comes on fast.

The governor is giving account of his administration. He
talks in front of a floodlit screen. When he needs to explain a
point of finance he has the figures thrown on the screen from
a slide. He's explaining his budget to the public. He has a
clear sharp way of putting things. While he does occasionally
pull out the organ notes of the professional orator his story
hangs together; the public servant accounting to his constit-
uents.

Brazilian comicios, particularly in this mad campaign of '62,
never end. José Augusto says it's time to dine. Gradually the
chauffeur manages to back his car out of the crowd.

A full moon has risen above the Atlantic. Natal rises from
the sea in ranks of stucco cubes, theatrically lit by the street-
lights against a background of high black headlands. It is really
beautiful in the moonlight. We eat at the aviation officers
club, on a terrace overlooking an inlet. The place has the look
of having been built by the Americans twenty years back. We
are absolutely alone there except for a solitary figure at the
bar inside.

The waiter produces elegantly broiled slices of a large fish
I don't catch the name of. Lime and Bacardi. (Exiled from
Cuba, Bacardi rum is now produced in Recife.) After the
long drive and the dust and the crowded governor's palace and
the jampacked comicio the stillness is delicious, the emptiness, the moonlit water.

The figure at the bar turns out to be a local poet. He's been
at the bar a long time. He weaves down the terrace to greet
us. He hovers around the table. Talking, gesticulating, expos-
tulating, there seem to be three or four of him. I get the feeling the place is crowded. He shows an amazing knowledge of
North American writing. He loves Sherwood Anderson: *Poor
White, Winesburg, Ohio . . .*

Poor Sherwood, I'm thinking, so many years dead. How he would have enjoyed this scene. The unfamiliar inlet between mysterious hills in the moonlight. The empty terrace, the puzzled waiter; José Augusto, who's a proper young man, explaining apologetically that the gentleman really is a very good poet . . . How Sherwood Anderson would have enjoyed the scene and the drunken poet praising him.

We had to tear ourselves away in a hurry. My appointment with Bishop Sales was at nine and it suddenly transpired that his episcopal residence was not in Natal, but in a fishing village called Ponta Negra, fourteen kilometers away. Our suggestion to the chauffeur that we mustn't keep the bishop waiting, caused him to tear off at such speed through the complicated moonlit streets of Natal and along a narrow bumpy road that skirted a great moonwashed beach that I really thought he'd be the end of us. It was only when I explained to him that it was not extreme unction I was seeking from the bishop but an interview, that he saw the point and slowed down.

Bishop Sales has a dark eager aquiline countenance with just a touch of Savonarola. His spare frame has a vigorous athletic look under the black cassock. He sits on a small hard chair in his bare little office, talking with his legs crossed in a rather unecclesiastical manner.

His program to combat Communism, he says right away, is only one of a dozen programs in various parts of Brazil. It is not a program of religious propaganda, he insists. He wants to awaken a sense of human dignity and of the duties of citizenship in a democracy.

In furtherance of this general aim, he conducts courses in reading and writing: alphabetization, he calls it, over the radio.

He wants a Christian labor movement that will be independent of politicians and Communists and also of employer influences. He wants trade unions that will really stand up for the rights and dignity of labor.

Like Aluísio Alves his appeal is to the teenagers. Every week he invites a group of young people from interior towns and villages to spend three days at Ponta Negra for an indoctrination course. He furnishes them with small batterypowered radios to take home so that they can tune in on the lessons and lectures he broadcasts every day: alphabetization, hygiene, sanitation, simple information that people need in the back country. The young people tune in and explain the lessons to their parents.

He takes me into the next room, where a group of boys and girls, some of them so young they must still be in grade school, are peering at sentences written on a blackboard. Their faces shine when he addresses them. They are having fun, like boy or girl scouts in the States.

"See how they enjoy it," he says eagerly when we go back to his office. He pours me a glass of coconut water.

"Communist propaganda succeeds," he says, "because nobody has shown enough interest to talk to the people first. You see how they light up. They know I am interested in them."

He went on to lament the fact that many great Brazilian capitalists were so shortsighted—out of a mistaken nationalism perhaps—as to back Communist agitators. He regretted too that the U. S. State Department wouldn't subsidize any of the church programs for promoting the democratic faith. He needed all the help he could get. There was so much to be done.

The chauffeur drove us back to town at a snail's pace when I told him I wanted to enjoy the sight of the beach and the rocky coast in the moonlight. The enormous bed at the government guesthouse couldn't have been more comfortable. It had been a long day.

On the Road—September 15

José Augusto and I joined the governor's caravan in the
early morning at a flourishing sugar plantation near Ceará
Mirim some miles inland from Natal. The refinery was working. Smoke rose from its tall yellowbrick chimney. A wonderful little toy locomotive with a funnelshaped stack was shunting in little cars full of cane. The sort of little locomotive
you want to wrap up and take home.

Under the trees opposite, on a knoll that stood up out of
a glaucous ocean of cane that stretched to the horizon, cars
were stacked every which way against a big comfortable
house.

We found the party at breakfast. The dining room looked
like a Marriage at Cana by one of the more animated Vene-
tians. A variety of people ate, talked, argued, gesticulated
about a long table that groaned with dishes of fried eggs and
plates of ham and patties of manioc flour, all stacked about
a row of stately poundcakes down the middle. At one end
the blond hostess was pouring out oceans of coffee and hot
milk. At the other sat the large monsignor, his cassock en-
livened by a little red piping, who was the candidate for
Lieutenant-Governor. Maids rushed in and out with plates
and cups. New arrivals greeted each other with abraços. Precinct workers slid in and out with messages.

Outside, the geese in the courtyard kept up an uneasy
hissing, ducks quacked from a pool, children romped, drivers
raced the motors of their cars. Bem-ti-vís piped in the trees
overhead.

Eventually the governor emerged from a conference in a
back room. People were loaded into cars, handbags were
stowed away. Aluísio Alves, a green handkerchief in his hand,
took his place in the first car and we were off across the
countryside. In the first village there was a new school and

a new well to be inaugurated. The children had green scarves
and danced up and down chanting: "Aluísio, Aluísio." The
teachers and authorities stood beaming in the sun. On the
edge of the crowd boys set off rockets.

And so on, village by village, new schools, water systems,
public privies, speeches, singing school children, green bunting that lashed about in the seabreeze, until, at a palmthatched fisherman's hamlet near Cape São Roque we
changed to jeeps for a run along the coast.

Cruising in a jeep over the white beaches and the tawny
dunes was terrific. It was almost like being on skis. We
skimmed round the edges of dunes, past endless variations of
surf on shining sand, on rocky ledges; and blue sea and green
shallows and japanesy little villages under coconut palms
with canoes and jangadas ranked on the beach in front of
them.

This coast north of Natal is very beautiful but dreadfully
poor. Fish are scarce. The only reliable income comes from
crawfish which abound under the reefs and ledges. Only now
with new roads opening up is it profitable to market them.
Schemes are in the works to set up refrigerating equipment
so as to ship out the lobstertails for which the demand in
the world market seems endless.

At each village the governor visits the school. There's a
little parade through the sandy streets with the local authorities and precinct workers, and a speech, songs, cheers, flower-
petals scattered like confetti over the governor's head, rockets
and cherry bombs. The governor tells of his unsuccessful efforts to get equipment from the federal government for
schools and clinics, for road building, for water systems. (Actually he's working with the Alliance for Progress but he
doesn't make a point of it.) He points to the new public
privy or the deep well or the school he's built or repaired.
Some schools have gone without even having the walls
cleaned since the administration of Washingtón Luíz more

than thirty years ago. He tells how much there is to do. He makes a touching personal appeal. "If you are satisfied vote for the men who will help me; if not, vote against me."

We turned inland at a place on a clear palmfringed river called Rio do Fôgo. In a patch of richer appearing country with little plantations of papaya and manioc and banana we ate lunch at a long table in the breezeway of a wellkept schoolhouse in the midst of a great crowd of bystanders. The children and old men and women watched every mouthful. The staple here seems to be tapioca instead of rice. All along this coast they bring you green coconut water to drink, a delight because the sun is hot and the dust parching.

During the afternoon, having changed back to the cars that had come through back roads to meet us we drove through some of the most depressing inland country I had ever seen. Agave grown for fiber was the main crop. Often there was no other vegetation. The plantations were indicated by rows of dreary hovels with fiber in heaps beside them. Men, women, and children had a drab and dusty look.

We reach a real jumping off place, in the midst of a vast sunsmitten plain. Two straggles of dilapidated shacks form a sort of crossroads—only there isn't any real road—with a tin windmill to pump water at the intersection. The windmill has broken down. The broken parts are mournfully brought out for the governor's inspection.

The landowner looks almost as badly off as his tenants. "I wouldn't live here," he says with some bitterness, "except that it's the only land God saw fit to give me."

It was dark by the time we reached Touros. Touros was a goodsized fishing town on the beach. The people seemed full of beans. A band played. Floodlights lit the speakers' platform set up in the square across from a recent monument attractively contrived out of aluminum sheets to simulate a jangada. The firmament resounded with the explosion of rockets and, fortunately at some distance, behind the church, somebody set off bombs so loud they must have been sticks of dynamite.

Aluísio Alves was at his best. He told us about his last visit to Touros in the course of an unsuccessful campaign and how he got there late and the people waited all night to hear him, and how their friendliness had cheered him. He told of the three years of work that still lay ahead of him in his battle against disease and illiteracy. Eighty per cent couldn't read or write. Ninetyeight per cent suffered from schistosomiasis. Of every two children born, one child died in infancy. "People of Touros, with your help we shall change all this—our campaign is the campaign of hope." And the green pennants waved.

The governor and his party were to be put up in a small house perched on a sand dune. Half the population of Touros had gotten there ahead to receive us. In fact they had eaten up most of the dinner laid out on a variety of tables set end to end. About all that was left was a little spaghetti, still cold in the can. There was one chair for the governor, but no more.

The porches were full of boys and girls who had come from interior towns to the speaking. The problem was where people would sleep. There were no beds and few cots and hammocks. As the large monsignor and I were the oldest, we were assigned to the privacy of a tiny leanto which housed tools back of the house A cot was found for me and an effort was made to swing a hammock above it for the monsignor. Alas, we were both large men. There was no way of fitting us into the space. The monsignor handsomely retired and I was left alone. God knows where he slept. It was just as well I was out in the leanto because the racket in the house was indescribable. Everybody in town wanted to speak to the governor.

The governor went off to a dance given in his honor. He had addressed the crowd about two dozen times during the day. He had just finished a fulldress oration. He had driven eight or ten hours through the heat and the dust. He is a rather slight man. He must be made of iron.

Mossoró, September 16: the Long Long Sunday

A heavy shower of rain on the roof woke me at about four-thirty. When the rain stopped rockets started hissing up all around the house and exploding in the sky overhead. They have the loudest rockets in Touros I've ever heard. I mucked around in the yard behind the kitchen, awash with thin mud from the rain, in search of the washbasin. There was only one. Shaved among the awakening teenagers on the porch looking out on the long slow green spuming waves advancing towards the beach below the house out of a pearly ocean in the morning twilight.

Met our hosts. In the hubbub last night I didn't have a chance to sort them out. The reddish-haired stocky man must be the paterfamilias. There are various sons, one a young man on crutches. The two elderly women stoking up a small charcoal brazier in the kitchen must be the maids. Nobody seems to be disturbed by the house having been turned last night into something like the New York subway at rush hour. We have to admit that the accommodations are plain.

Sitting on packing boxes at the table the large monsignor and I are regaled with a breakfast of eggs, toasted cheese, black coffee, and bread. Couldn't be better.

Then we take an early morning stroll around the town in the governor's train. Touros looks more modest by day than it did in the light of the floodlights. Squarish blocks of stucco houses. Sand in the streets. These strolls around town accompanied by the local authorities are part of the program at each place we stop. Anybody who feels like it comes up to speak to the governor. He listens to them all, old and young, rich and poor. He listens with a serious air, with an occasional wry smile. If it's a matter of some detail a secretary steps up to take notes. Aluísio Alves is a man of few words except when he is delivering a speech.

The mayor of Touros wants us to visit the school but it's Sunday and no one can find the key. At last an intelligent-looking old woman arrives breathless. Everybody helps her as the big key is hard to turn and the doubledoors stick. She must be over seventy but I think she's the schoolteacher.

By the time we have toured the schoolrooms the cars have lined up outside. Governor Alves gets into the seat next the chauffeur with his green handkerchief fluttering and we are off. It is a long drive, over a decent gravel road that shows signs of fresh repairs, to what I'm told is the world's largest agave plantation. The company has an English name. There is an endless row of company houses—all alike, bleak, un-shaded, of cracked stucco—but the fact that they are houses is a cause for admiration. There are long warehouses, piles of sisal drying (this is not hennequen but an agave that pro-duces a very similar fiber), and an airstrip.

Two small planes, one the governor's Cessna, are waiting for us. Those who can't fit into the planes will follow by road. When we take off we can really appreciate the immen-sity of the plantation. A checkerboard of the spinyleaved agaves spreads in every direction over the rolling hills. We fly inland.

At São Miguel the country is even hillier. The people wait-ing for us at the airstrip are welldressed. Everything looks more prosperous. Abraços, felicidades. Great enthusiasm. This is the township where Aluísio Alves was born. Local boy makes good. Every face beams with a personal pride in him. We are driven into town. The greeting throng follows in a truck, a few of them on sleek caramelcolored ponies.

This is the longstaple cotton region. Perennial cotton was introduced by British companies some forty years ago. The country looks like Arizona with rosy desert mesas and flower-like formations of gray rock. The air is dry. There is a crispness to the breeze although the sun is plumb overhead.

At São Miguel we sit at a table with a clean cloth and eat a second—or is it a third?—breakfast. When someone speaks of more milk, the girl who is waiting on us smilingly brings in a large pitcher of milk from the electric refrigerator in the back room. On the coast where we were nobody would have dreamed of milk. That pitcher of milk is more eloquent than a dozen speeches. After the sight of such poverty it is a real pleasure to be among prosperous people again.

After São Miguel we were driven over to another prosperous looking town, Pedro Pedrosa. Milk on sale in the market, and eggs, and decentlooking meat. Few flies. While Governor Alves was addressing the crowd a young man in riding boots invited me in perfect English to have a drink with him. He professed great admiration for Governor Alves. He had been several times to the States. He was the soninlaw of the man who owned a large part of the local cotton business. He was full of the possibilities of developing this region into one of the great longstaple cotton producers of the world. He wanted American capital. He'd spoken to a Rockefeller. "For God's sake," he said, "go home and tell the people in Washington to eliminate Castro . . . It is Castro that is the roadblock against progress in the Northeast."

The air was bumpy to Martins, an ancient little city perched on a green cultivated ridge high above the arid hills. Martins is the highest populated area in the state. At two thousand feet the altitude gives it a climate of its own. We found the sun roasting, but the wind cool. There were flower-

ing trees and cobbled squares flanked by the long barred
windows and tall green blinds of colonial buildings.

A dam was to be inaugurated. The cavalcade of cars
plunged through the clinging dust to the edge of a lake in
the valley below. It was long after noon. The speakers were
grouped on a ranch wagon under the full lash of the sun. The
governor spoke. The visitors spoke. The candidates spoke.
The local authorities spoke. From the broiling crowd came
questions and enthusiastic responses. At last after a couple
of hours we were driven back into town to the cool airy corridors of the maternity hospital.

There the ladies' auxiliary, so much like the ladies who
would serve a meal for the benefit of a church or the PTA in
any North American rural community, served a magnificent
lunch (for the benefit of the hospital)—roast beef, chicken
with rice, venison, an assortment of rolled meats and meat
balls variously seasoned and sprinkled with *farinha*—washed
down by pitcher after pitcher of coconut water and a special
soft beverage flavored with guava. The guava filled the room
with a sort of strawberry fragrance.

From Martins the flight was smooth through horizontal
sunlight to Mossoró. Mossoró is the second city in the state.
The drive in from the airport is a nightmare of noise. Three
or four cars abreast, trucks and jeeps move in a slow roaring
traffic jam into town. Every horn and claxon is sounding
two notes from the governor's campaign song: "Aluísio,
Aluísio."

This comicio is dedicated to the *meninos*, the children of
the city. The motorcade stalls on a street leading into the
square. A parade has become entangled with the traffic jam.
There are ranks of girls and boys in costume, marching
bands, drum majorettes.

In front of the reviewing stand in the square two floats are
stranded. On one is seated a young lady dressed like the

Statue of Liberty. She's already tired of holding up her torch. On the other, a plump youth stripped to the shorts is bound to a plaster pillar by newlooking aluminum chains to represent servitude. Although it's obviously been a long day he's still holding up his manacled hands with right good will.

Seeing that I look rather parched after listening to so many speeches in so much sun a thin man with a gray mustache from city hall leads me into the corner bar for a beer. The bar is full of hardbitten characters, obviously not meninos, who are taking advantage of the festivities to get thoroughly tanked up. We are latched onto by the inevitable grubby drunk who thinks he can speak English. He worked for the American submarine base during the war. He loves Americans.

The governor's chauffeur, a thicknecked man who has the look that bodyguards have the world over—Lacerda would have called him "a sort of Gregório"—comes to fetch us. The speeches are about to start. He tactfully disentangles us from the drunk who loves Americans.

Indeed the children of Mossoró have turned out. Babes in arms, toddlers in their gauzy best. All the pretty girls. Boys and men perch like starlings in the trees of the jampacked square.

The afternoon is absolutely airless. The stand is crowded tight. Every menino who wants to is encouraged to climb up on it. It is hard to pay attention to the speakers on account of the squirming and the wriggling and the squeezing and the shuffling of the little ones working their way between the legs of the assembled politicos. Each one wants to get near the governor.

The boards of the stand creak. I'm wondering if they'll bear the weight.

Beside me a gentleman in a white suit for whom no time has been found on the program is angrily jumping up and down as he argues with some official. The stand sways and groans. I'm expecting the scantlings to give way any minute.

The speeches go on and on. Every local politico has his say. A gentleman named Duarte Filho is running for prefeito. Evidently the campaign is violent in Mossoró because the denunciations of the opposition become more and more extreme as twilight falls. There are too many adults among the children in the square. Toughlooking waterfront characters like the men in the bar. I'm worried about what would happen to all the little children if the meeting should end in a brawl.

While I'm trying to catch what the speakers are shouting a skinny grayhaired man, shoved up against my midriff by the crowd on the stand, pours into my ear a story you could hear only in Brazil. He too worked at the American submarine base. He too likes Americans. He knows a cave where there are crystals that shine bright as the headlights of a car. He has samples at his home. If they aren't diamonds they are something just as valuable. He wants me to tell him the name of an American engineer. Brazilian engineers don't have the education to exploit such a treasure or else they will try to steal it all for themselves. Can't I find him an American engineer to prospect the cave? Diamonds as big as your fist shine with their own light in the darkness.

The square grows dark. The closepacked crowd is getting hotter and hotter. On the stand we sweat rivers. Speeches are becoming more and more violent. Men in the crowd have a threatening look. A dangerous tension seems to be building up. Suddenly a samba band begins to play.

I've been noticing one small band that officials have been trying to keep quiet, behind the speakers' stand, shushing and pushing back the dark boys with instruments. The minute the governor stops talking they won't be shushed any longer. Their drums throb. The sound of sambas rises from every street that leads into the square.

In three minutes half the people are dancing. The oratory

fades away. No more traffic jam. The floats are moving. The meeting turns into a sort of carnival parade with samba schools dancing ahead of the floats, each behind its own banner. TOO YOUNG TO VOTE, reads one. Songs take the place of speeches. Children, teenagers, old men and women, everybody is dancing.

No more tension. A cool breeze seems to sweep through the streets. The young kids are marvelous. In front of Duarte Filho's house it is like a ballet. I've never seen such really beautiful dancing as fills the streets of Mossoró for hours, far into the night.

The governor and his party have gone on to another comicio. Don't they ever get tired? I can still hear the piping and throbbing of distant sambas drifting in through the window of the pleasant old tropical hotel—there's a shower, and a clean bed and the trade wind through the louvers, and even a reading light—what more could you want?—as I drift off to sleep.